17-26-32

THE LAW COMMISSION

WORKING PAPER NO. 79

OFFENCES AGAINST RELIGION AND PUBLIC WORSHIP

CONTENTS

(iii)

(v)

THE LAW COMMISSION

Working Paper No. 79

OFFENCES AGAINST RELIGION AND PUBLIC WORSHIP

I INTRODUCTION

1.1   Offences against religion and offences against
public worship form a small group of crimes of great antiquity
which have connections, on the one hand, with offences against
public order, and on the other, with offences of obscenity and
indecency. Nevertheless, they do not fit easily into either
of these categories of offence and usually receive separate
treatment in the standard works on the criminal law.[1] As
part of its programme for examining the criminal law with
the object of producing a criminal code, the Law Commission
has undertaken to review these offences, and the present
Working Paper sets out its provisional proposals for reform.

1.2   At the outset of this Paper it is necessary to
emphasise that common law offences, that is, offences the
elements of which are defined by reference to judicial
decision rather than legislation, can have no place in a
modern codification of the law. Much of the law in this area,
in particular the offences of blasphemy and blasphemous
libel, is still governed by the common law. Our review

---

1   See e.g. Archbold, Criminal Pleading Evidence and
       Practice (40th ed., 1979), Ch. 23; Russell on Crime
       (12th ed., 1964), Vol. 2, Pt. 12; Halsbury's Laws of
       England (4th ed., 1976) Vol. 11, paras. 1009-1010.

of these offences therefore presupposes that they cannot be
left in their present state. Our task is to examine all of
them with a view to ascertaining whether they need be retained
and, if so, whether it would be satisfactory merely to
substitute for the present law new, statutory offences
embodying the substance of the common law, or whether an
entirely new approach would be desirable.

1.3   The Paper gives separate consideration to offences
against public worship, which are dealt with in Part XII, and
offences against religion. Of the latter, the common law
offences of blasphemy and its written form of blasphemous
libel are the most important and occupy the greater part of
this Paper. It should be noted that the law relating to other
forms of libel attracting criminal penalties is under
separate review.[2]

II   DEVELOPMENT OF THE LAW OF BLASPHEMY AND BLASPHEMOUS LIBEL

2.1   According to the trial judge in the recent case of
Whitehouse v. Lemon, blasphemous libel is committed if there
is published any writing concerning God or Christ, the
Christian religion, the Bible, or some sacred subject, using
words which are scurrilous, abusive or offensive and which
tend to vilify the Christian religion and therefore have a

---

2   Criminal libel is the subject of a separate study by the
    Law Commission and proposals for reform of this offence
    will be contained in a Working Paper to be issued shortly.
    Seditious libel was examined in the Commission's
    Working Paper No. 72 (1977) Treason, Sedition and Allied
    Offences. Obscene libel, which so long as the Obscene
    Publications Act 1959 is in force may not be charged in
    respect of any article as therein defined (see ss. 1(2),
    2(4) and 2(4)(A)), would be abolished if the
    recommendations of the Williams Committee Report on
    Obscenity and Film Censorship (1979) Cmnd. 7772 were
    implemented; see further para. 5.4, below.

tendency to lead to a breach of the peace.[3] In the House of Lords in the same case Lord Scarman approved at the end of his speech[4] the following definition taken from Stephen's Digest -

> "Every publication is said to be blasphemous which contains any contemptuous, reviling, scurrilous or ludicrous matter relating to God, Jesus Christ, or the Bible, or the formularies of the Church of England as by law established. It is not blasphemous to speak or publish opinions hostile to the Christian religion, or to deny the existence of God, if the publication is couched in decent and temperate language. The test to be applied is as to the manner in which the doctrines are advocated and not as to the substance of the doctrines themselves. Everyone who publishes any blasphemous document is guilty ... of publishing a blasphemous libel. Everyone who speaks blasphemous words is guilty of... blasphemy".

Both of these definitions emphasise the strongly offensive character which material must possess in order for it to be penalised by the common law offence, which distinguishes the legal definition of blasphemy from its very much wider dictionary meaning.[5] Moreover, both definitions are consistent, save that the trial judge included as part of his direction some element of a tendency towards a breach of the peace.[6] But

---

3   This summarises the elements of blasphemous libel set out in the summing-up by Judge King-Hamilton Q.C. in R. v. Lemon, R. v. Gay News Ltd., Central Criminal Court, 11 July 1977 (transcript, p.9). Neither the Court of Appeal (R. v. Lemon, R. v. Gay News Ltd. [1979] Q.B. 10) nor members of the House of Lords other than Lord Scarman (Whitehouse v. Lemon, Whitehouse v. Gay News Ltd. [1979] A.C. 617) attempted a compendious definition of blasphemous libel.

4   [1979] A.C. 617, 665-666, quoting Stephen's Digest of the Criminal Law (9th ed., 1950), Article 214.

5   The dictionary definition of blasphemy includes any "impious or profane talk" (Concise Oxford Dictionary, 6th ed., 1976); see further para. 7.2, below.

6   See paras. 2.14 and 3.3-3.4, below.

whichever definition is preferred, they obviously raise
questions as to the precise ambit of the offence, which can
only be answered by a proper understanding of the way in which
the law has developed up to the present; thus we consider it
essential to examine the history of the offence in this part
of the Working Paper (paragaphs 2.2-2.25). It should be
emphasised that this is no more than an outline of the
principal developments, citing only those cases which appear
to us to be significant in the development of the law. In
most of these cases we do not find it useful to give details
of the facts since, although in many instances they indicate
what was regarded as shocking to contemporary juries, social
changes render them of no more than historical interest.
Moreover, quotation from material found to be blasphemous in
more recent cases is not possible without repeating the
offence.[7] The development of the law is followed by a detailed
examination of how the law stands today (Part III). Discussion
of the shortcomings of the present law and how it might be
reformed (Parts VI - VIII) is preceded by a review of the law
in other countries and of other offences which may be charged
in order to penalise blasphemous conduct (Parts IV and V).

A. The common law, 1676-1922

2.2   "Taylor's Case[8] is the foundation stone of this part
of the law",[9] and the authority of that case has recently been
confirmed.[10] Blasphemy was originally an ecclesiastical
offence punishable in the ecclesiastical courts, but by the
end of the 17th century the sanctions which could be imposed
by those courts had lost their effectiveness, while other
courts capable of dealing with religious offences (the Court of

---

7   See the Law of Libel Amendment Act 1888, s.3 (proviso),
     para. 3.7, below.

8   (1676) 1 Vent. 293;   86 E.R. 189.

9   Bowman v. Secular Society Ltd. [1917] A.C. 406, 457 per
     Lord Sumner.

10   R. v. Lemon [1979] Q.B. 10, 21 and 23 per Roskill L.J.

4

Star Chamber and the Court of High Commission) had been abolished. The Court of King's Bench filled this gap and Taylor was the first reported case.[11] Objection was taken that the offence charged was an ecclesiastical one, and it also seems that some attempt was made by the defendant to say that the offending words were not meant in their literal sense. The indictment, however, showed that the defendant's language was not only contrary to religion but was also regarded as constituting a danger to civil order; and Hale C.J. affirmed that "such kind of wicked blasphemous words were not only an offence to God and religion, but a crime against the laws, State and Government, and therefore punishable in this Court". He added his famous dictum that "Christianity is parcel of the laws of England", a statement which was only finally disapproved over two hundred years later,[12] but the case remains authority for blasphemy being an offence at common law, in which evidence of the defendant's intent in publishing the words concerned is irrelevant and therefore inadmissible.

2.3   There followed many prosecutions during the 18th century where the matters complained of included attacks on the Deity or the Bible or the Christian religion in general. At this time however there were no rigid criteria to distinguish the classes of criminal words which were the subject of libel charges; there was an overlap between seditious and blasphemous libel in that where the object of the offending words was the officials or the government of the established Church, it was described as seditious, but where it was the Deity or the Bible, as blasphemous.[13] The lack of any clear dividing line reflected the fact that the State's primary interest was its own security. Consequently

---

11   Perhaps not the first case, but this remains unclear; see Nokes, A History of the Crime of Blasphemy (1928) pp. 42-53, and Leigh, "Not to judge but to save" (1978) Cambrian L.R. p. 56.

12   R. v. Ramsay and Foote (1883) 15 Cox C.C. 231, 235 per Lord Coleridge C.J.

13   Nokes, op. cit., p. 76; Whitehouse v. Lemon [1979] A.C. 617, 633-634 per Lord Diplock.

the State intervened by using the criminal law to punish those whose attacks on Christianity or the Deity were regarded as a menace to the foundations of the established religion and thus to society in general. It is therefore not surprising that the number of prosecutions increased during the disturbed period following the French Revolution for fear that the denial of Christian truths in such a work as Paine's Age of Reason might give rise to civil disturbance.

2.4 Nevertheless there were influences at work at the turn of the 18th century which fundamentally affected the law as it now stands. Fox's Libel Act, "An Act to remove Doubts respecting the Functions of Juries in Cases of Libel", was passed in 1792. Prior to that date it was for the judge to rule as a matter of law whether published matter alleged to constitute a blasphemous libel was indeed blasphemous; the Act enabled the jury to give their verdict on this, as well as on the issue of publication, both as matters of fact. It should be noted that the Act did not distinguish between seditious and blasphemous libel. Probably as a result of this Act directions to the jury during the first half of the 19th century allowed that temperate discussion of the truth of Christianity was not in itself indictable. Certainly, text writers early in that century[14] moved towards the view that reasonable discussion of the fundamentals of religion would not of itself be an offence. This view found its most authoritative expression in the writings of Starkie who, in his influential textbook on the law of libel, set out the old view of the law, and continued[15] -

> "There can be no doubt as to the general right
> of inquiry and discussion even upon the most
> sacred subjects, provided the licence be exercised
> in the spirit of temperance, moderation, and
> fairness, without any intention to injure or
> affront .... It cannot be doubted that any man

---

14 E.g. Holt, The Law of Libel (1816), p. 70; see Nokes
     op. cit. at p. 92.

15 Treatise on the Law of Slander and Libel (2nd ed.,
     1830) p. 146.

has a right, not merely to judge for himself
on [the questions of the relations between the
Creator and the beings of his creation], but also
legally speaking to publish his opinions for the
benefit of others."

2.5   From the legal viewpoint, the most significant of
the cases in the first half of the 19th century, if only for
the reliance which has recently been placed on it, was R. v.
Hetherington, where a charge of blasphemous libel was brought
against a radical publisher. In the course of his summing-up
Lord Denman C.J. said[16] -

"even discussions upon [the great doctrines of
Christianity itself] may be by no means a matter
of criminal prosecution but, if they be carried
on in a sober and temperate and decent style,
even those discussions may be tolerated and may
take place without criminality attaching to
them; but ... if the tone and spirit is that
of offence and insult and ridicule, which
leaves the judgment really not free to act and
therefore cannot be truly called an appeal to
the judgment, but an appeal to the wild and
improper feelings of the human mind, more
particularly in the younger part of the community,
in that case the jury will hardly feel it possible
to say that such opinions so expressed do not
deserve the character which is affixed to them
in this indictment. With that general observation,
I leave the question of libel to you. Is it, or
is it not, a blasphemous libel which the defendant
appears to have published in his shop?"

Temperate discussion of the truth of Christianity was therefore
not to be prosecuted for blasphemy; but at any rate in the
case of a publisher, the question for the jury was still
"blasphemous libel or not?"[17]

---

16   (1841) 4 St. Tr. N.S. 563, 590.

17   "The only question for you to decide is a matter of fact
and opinion. Aye or not, is this in your opinion a
blasphemous publication and has the defendant ... issued
it knowingly and wilfully?", ibid., at p. 593, cited in
Whitehouse v. Lemon [1979] Q.B. 10, 23 and 27 (C.A.) and
[1979] A.C. 617, 663 where Lord Scarman stated that in
this context "'wilfully' meant no more than 'deliberately'."

2.6   At that time the position of the publisher in the criminal law of libel (including blasphemous libel) was affected by the fact that a man was responsible for the publication of a libel by his agent even though he had not personally authorised it.[18] Thus it followed that in the case of a publisher the only appropriate question for the jury was, as we have noted, "blasphemous libel or not?" But after prolonged pressure by newspaper publishers worried by prosecutions for criminal libel, the publisher's position was ameliorated by section 7 of the Libel Act 1843, which is still in force. It provides that, when a defendant pleads not guilty to the publication of a libel, evidence which establishes a "presumptive case" of publication against him "by the act of any other person by his authority" may be rebutted by him on proof of evidence "that such publication was made without his authority, consent or knowledge, and that the said publication did not arise from want of due care or caution on his part."

2.7   While it is clear from Hetherington[19] that a publication was to be regarded as blasphemous only if "the tone and spirit is that of offence and insult and ridicule", it is less clear to what extent an intent to blaspheme was a necessary element of the offence. This was indeed the issue for decision by the House of Lords in Whitehouse v. Lemon.[20] Certainly the language of intention is to be found in cases from the early part of the century; for example, in R. v. Richard Carlile[21] Lord Abbott C.J. directed the jury in the

---

18 See generally on this aspect J.R. Spencer, "The Press and the Reform of Criminal Libel" in Reshaping the Criminal Law (1978) at p. 273, Buxton "The Case of Blasphemous Libel" [1978] Crim. L.R. 673 and Whitehouse v. Lemon [1979] A.C. 617 at p. 650 per Lord Edmund-Davies.

19 (1841) 4 St. Tr. N.S. 563; see para. 2.5, above.

20 [1979] A.C. 617.

21 (1819) 1 St. Tr. N.S. 1387.

following terms -

> "It will be for you to say whether in anything you have heard from the defendant you can find anything enabling you to say that the defendant did not at the time he published this intend to bring the Christian religion into disbelief and contempt. If he did, that is an unlawful intention and it appears to me that you ought on your consciences to pronounce him guilty."[22]

Shortly afterwards, Starkie, after stating in terms already quoted[23] that temperate discussion of religious truths was permissible, continued -

> "It is the mischievous abuse of this state of intellectual liberty which calls for penal censure. The law visits not the honest errors, but the malice of mankind. A wilful intention to pervert, insult, and mislead others, by means of licentious and contumelious abuse applied to sacred subjects, or by wilful misrepresentations or wilful sophistry, calculated to mislead the ignorant and unwary, is the criterion and test of guilt. A malicious and mischievous intention, or what is equivalent to such an intention, in law, as well as morals - a state of apathy and indifference to the interests of society - is the broad boundary between right and wrong."[24]

2.8   It may well be that, however this passage is interpreted - and this was the subject of extended consideration in <u>Whitehouse</u> v. <u>Lemon</u>[25] - Starkie's proposition was somewhat in advance of its time and that, as Lord Diplock observed, the language "is perhaps more that of the advocate of law reform than of the draftsman of a criminal code."[26]

---

22   <u>Ibid.</u>, at p. 1390. We comment further in para. 2.10, below on the significance of the defendant giving evidence in this and other cases in this period.

23   See para. 2.4, above.

24   <u>Treatise on the Law of Slander and Libel</u>   (2nd ed., 1830) p. 146.

25   [1979] Q.B. 10 (C.A.) and [1979] A.C. 617 and see paras. 2.15-2.22, below.

26   <u>Ibid.</u>, at p. 635. Starkie was one of the Criminal Law Commissioners in the 1830's and 1840's and was co-draftsman with Lord Campbell of the Libel Act 1843 (as to which, see para. 2.6, above).

Certainly, the references therein to "intention" were, as we
have seen, not reflected in the summing up in Hetherington.[27]
But the importance of Starkie's proposition was felt fully in
R. v. Ramsay and Foote[28] and in R. v. Bradlaugh[29] which in
1883 rejected decisively the old view that any discussion of
the fundamentals of Christianity could by itself found a
prosecution for blasphemy, and in doing so went far to define
the ambit of the law for the future. In the former case
Lord Coleridge C.J. denied that Christianity was part of the
law[30] and told the jury that "to asperse the truth of
Christianity cannot per se be sufficient to sustain a criminal
prosecution for blasphemy"; and went on -

> "I now lay it down as law, that, if the decencies
> of controversy are observed, even the fundamentals
> of religion may be attacked without the writer
> being guilty of blasphemy." [31]

Essentially, this did no more than clarify and state in more
emphatic terms the law as laid down in Hetherington. But more
importantly, in both trials Starkie's dictum quoted in
paragraph 2.7 above, which included a requirement of intention,

---

27 (1841) 4 St. Tr. N.S. 563; see para. 2.5, above.

28 (1883) 15 Cox C.C. 231. It should be noted that in the
    interim, the Criminal Code Commissioners had reported:
    (1879) C. 2345. Sect. 141 of the draft Code provided for
    a maximum of one year's imprisonment for publication of
    a blasphemous libel. Whether or not any particular matter
    was a blasphemous libel was a matter of fact; "Provided
    that no one shall be liable to be convicted upon any
    indictment for a blasphemous libel only for expressing in
    good faith and in decent language, or attempting to
    establish by arguments used in good faith and conveyed in
    decent language, any opinion whatever upon any religious
    subject." Thus intent to blaspheme was not explicitly
    made an element of the offence under this provision. The
    Criminal Code Commissioners stated that "the law was stated
    by Mr. Justice Coleridge [father of Lord Coleridge C.J.]
    to this effect in the case of R. v. Pooley, [(1857) 8 St.
    Tr. N.S. 1089] tried at Bodmin in 1857."

29 (1883) 15 Cox C.C. 217.

30 R. v. Ramsay and Foote (1883) 15 Cox C.C. 231, 235.

31 Ibid., at p. 238.

was read out and approved by Lord Coleridge as "a correct statement of the law".[32] And in Bradlaugh he directed the jury that the question for their consideration was whether the indicted libels -

> "are not calculated and intended to insult the feelings and the deepest religious convictions of the great majority of the persons amongst whom we live."[33]

These two cases thus embodied an apparently unqualified judicial recognition of the intention to shock believers, with a consequent reflection on what was capable of being blasphemous matter.

2.9   Whether the judicial recognition of the intent to shock believers in these important cases was indeed unqualified has to be assessed against the background of contemporary rules of practice and procedure. It was not until the enactment of section 1 of the Criminal Evidence Act 1898 that an accused was in general[34] competent to testify in his own defence. Prior to 1898, he could not go into the witness-box and give evidence. Thus in trials for blasphemy in the 19th century an accused would have been unable to testify to the jury as to his intention. If his intention had been in issue at all, it could only have been inferred from the words used and by the application of the presumption that a man intends the natural and probable consequences of his acts,[35] itself perhaps stemming from the incompetence of an accused to testify. Thus at the time of Ramsay and Foote and Bradlaugh, the question whether an accused had an intent to shock believers or not was a matter which, subject to the

---

32 15 Cox C.C. at pp. 226, 236.

33 (1883) 15 Cox C.C. 217, 230; the significance of the reference here to the "feelings" of others is discussed in n. 308, below.

34 There were a number of provisions permitting an accused to testify on oath in relation to specific statutory offences enacted between 1872 and 1898, such as the Criminal Law Amendment Act 1885.

35 See now Criminal Justice Act 1967, s.8 and n.103, below.

11

qualification to which we refer below,[36] could only have been inferred from the publication by applying the presumption. If the words published had, viewed objectively, the tendency to shock, "the application of the presumption was sufficient to convert this objective tendency into the actual intention of the accused."[37] Thus in the view of Lord Diplock in Whitehouse v. Lemon -

> "the distinction was often blurred between the tendency of the published words to produce a particular effect upon those to whom they were published and the intention of the publisher to produce that effect."[38]

2.10   It should be noted that the rigour of the rule which prevented an accused testifying on oath from the witness-box was in earlier 19th century cases ameliorated by the frequency with which those accused of blasphemy conducted their own defence and by their right to make an unsworn statement from the dock.[39] This gave them the opportunity of indicating their intention in publishing[40] and explains the references in summings-up at this time, to which we have already drawn attention,[41] to the opportunity given to the jury to assess the intention of the accused from what he himself had said.

2.11   The significance of the procedural rules which we have outlined, and, in the light of those rules, the

---

36 See para. 2.10.

37 Whitehouse v. Lemon [1979] A.C. 617, 636 per Lord Diplock.

38 Ibid., at p. 634.

39 As to the question of the circumstances in which this right could be exercised, see Cowan and Carter, "Unsworn Statements by Accused Persons" in Essays on the Law of Evidence (1956) pp. 205 et seq.

40 See Whitehouse v. Lemon [1979] A.C. 617, 663 per Lord Scarman.

41 See e.g. R. v. Richard Carlile (1819) 1 St. Tr. N.S. 1387 and para. 2.7, above.

interpretation to be put upon the dicta of Lord Coleridge C.J. in Ramsay and Foote[42] and Bradlaugh,[43] were among the more important matters examined by the House of Lords in Whitehouse v. Lemon[44] in the course of its consideration of the issue of intent in the law of blasphemy. We examine this case in more detail below.[45] It is sufficient here to note that the majority, agreeing with Viscount Dilhorne,[46] considered the procedural rules and the change upon them effected by the Criminal Evidence Act 1898 to be entirely irrelevant. In their view it was not necessary to consider the means by which the intent of an accused to blaspheme was established in earlier cases, since such an intent was never a necessary element of the offence. Those in the minority,[47] however, found these factors of importance in establishing what they considered to be the necessary elements of the offence today.

2.12   Whatever view is taken of the significance of Lord Coleridge's emphatic approval of the passage from Starkie quoted above in Ramsay and Foote and Bradlaugh, later authority[48] followed his dictum that "if the decencies

---

42   (1883) 15 Cox C.C. 231; see para. 2.8, above.

43   (1883) 15 Cox C.C. 217; see para. 2.8, above.

44   [1979] A.C. 617.

45   See para. 2.15, below.

46   See [1979] A.C. 617, 642.

47   See [1979] A.C. 617, 634 and 636 per Lord Diplock and 655 per Lord Edmund-Davies.

48   E.g. R. v. Boulter (1908) 72 J.P. 188, a case of blasphemy; compare Pankhurst v. Thompson (1886) 3 T.L.R. 199, 200. The law as decided in R. v. Ramsay and Foote was also applied in various unreported cases e.g. R. v. Stewart, 5 December 1911 (West Riding Assizes, Horridge J.); R. v. Bullock, 24 July 1912 (Leeds Assizes, Bankes J.): see H.B. Bonner, Penalties Upon Opinion (3rd ed., 1934), pp. 122 et seq.

of controversy are observed, even the fundamentals of religion may be attacked without the writer being guilty of blasphemy"[49]. The correctness of his direction to the jury in this respect was affirmed by the Court of Appeal[50] and House of Lords in Bowman v. Secular Society Ltd.,[51] a civil case which nonetheless necessitated consideration of the elements of the crime of blasphemy. In addition to affirming the authority of Lord Coleridge's dicta, the speeches in the House of Lords emphasised the offensive character of the subject-matter necessary for a charge of the offence. Thus Lord Parker of Waddington said it "involves a denial of or an attack upon some of the fundamental doctrines of the Christian religion" and that "to constitute blasphemy at common law there must be such an element of vilification, ridicule, or irreverence as would be likely to exasperate the feelings of others and so lead to a breach of the peace".[52] Lord Buckmaster commented[53] that "it is a striking fact that with one possible exception - the case of R. v. Woolston[54] - every reported case upon the matter, beginning with R. v. Taylor,[55] and continuing down to R. v. Ramsay[56] and R. v. Boulter,[57] is a case where the

---

49 Stephen resisted this "milder view of the law" in his writings; and see his History of the Criminal Law of England (1883) Vol. II, pp. 469-476.

50 Secular Society Ltd. v. Bowman [1915] 2 Ch. 447, 462 per Lord Cozens-Hardy M.R.

51 [1917] A.C. 406, 423 per Lord Finlay L.C., 433 per Lord Dunedin, 460 per Lord Sumner, 470 per Lord Buckmaster.

52 Ibid., at pp. 445-446.

53 Ibid., p. 470; see also Lord Sumner at 466-467.

54 (1729) Fitzg. 64, 1 Barn. K.B. 162; 94 E.R. 112 and 655. A clergyman published discourses maintaining that the miracles were to be taken allegorically rather than literally.

55 (1676) 1 Vent. 293, 86 E.R. 189; see para. 2.2, above.

56 (1883) 15 Cox C.C. 231; see para. 2.8, above.

57 (1908) 72 J.P. 188; see n. 48, above.

offence alleged was associated with, and I think constituted by, violent, offensive or indecent words".

2.13   It is noteworthy that Lord Parker affirmed that a tendency to a breach of the peace was one element of the offence.[58] From its context it is clear that Lord Parker intended "breach of the peace" to be understood in its traditional and longstanding sense,[59] which does not necessarily signify general disorder and includes any situation where there is danger to the person, for example, an assault or threatened assault by one person on another. But we have noted[60] that the proliferation of blasphemy cases in the late 18th and early 19th century took place against a background of fear of more general public disturbance, endangering the security of the State; the authorities were not concerned with mere individuals quarrelling in public. It was to this background that Lord Sumner referred when he said that -

> "Our Courts of law, in the exercise of their jurisdiction, do not, and never did that I can find, punish irreligious words as offences against God.... They dealt with such words for their manner, their violence, or ribaldry, or more fully stated, for their tendency to endanger the peace then and there, to deprave public morality generally, to shake the fabric of society, and to be a cause of civil strife. The words, as well as the acts, which tend to endanger society differ from time to time in proportion as society is stable or insecure in fact, or is believed by its reasonable members to be open to assault [and] in the present day reasonable men do not apprehend the dissolution or the downfall of society because religion is

---

58   See Lord Parker's definition quoted in para. 2.12, above.
59   See generally Glanville Williams "Arrest for Breach of the Peace" [1954] Crim. L.R. 578 at pp. 578-583.
60   See para. 2.3, above.

publicly assailed by methods not scandalous....
The question whether a given opinion is a danger
to society is a question of the times and is
a question of fact".[61]

In pointing out that what will endanger society will vary
from time to time, it is therefore clear that, by his
reference to a "tendency to endanger the peace", Lord
Sumner had in mind a concept different from and far wider
than that contained in Lord Parker's assertion that to
constitute blasphemy the matter complained of must be
"likely to exasperate the feelings of others and so lead
to a breach of the peace". This was made explicit in
Lord Sumner's comment that -

> "the gist of the offence of blasphemy is a
> supposed tendency in fact to shake the fabric
> of society generally. Its tendency to
> provoke an immediate breach of the peace is
> not the essential, but only an occasional
> feature".[62]

And it was this wider concept to which Lord Denning
referred when in 1949 he stated that -

> "The reason for this [blasphemy] law was
> because it was thought that a denial of
> Christianity was liable to shake the
> fabric of society, which was itself
> founded on the Christian religion. There
> is no such danger to society now and the
> offence of blasphemy is a dead letter".[63]

2.14   Nevertheless it was the more limited scope of the
term "a tendency to a breach of the peace", derived from
Lord Parker's speech, which was stressed as an element of

---

61   Bowman v. Secular Society Ltd. [1917] A.C. 406, 466-467;
     see further, n. 352, below.
62   Ibid., at pp. 459-460; and see Whitehouse v. Lemon
     [1979] Q.B. 10, 19 (C.A.).
63   Freedom Under the Law, Hamlyn Lectures, 1st series,
     1949, p. 46.

the offence in R. v. Gott,[64] the last reported case in the 20th century until the prosecution in Whitehouse v. Lemon in 1977. Furthermore, in his summing up Avory J. made it clear that there need be no evidence that a breach of the peace had occurred at the time of the publication of the offending words.[65] Nevertheless by contrast with Whitehouse v. Lemon there was some evidence that the sale in a public street of the pamphlet in respect of which the defendant was indicted did lead to some public altercation.[66]

B. Whitehouse v. Lemon

2.15   The years 1922-1977 saw no successful prosecutions for blasphemous libel. But the 1970's saw

---

64 (1922) 16 Cr. App. R. 87; the direction to the jury by Avory J. and the judgment of the Court of Criminal Appeal are fully reported in "The Freethinker", 8 January 1922, p. 28, 29 January 1922 pp. 75 and 91, and 12 February 1922, p. 109. The defendant was sentenced to nine months' hard labour.

65 Ibid., at p. 88. In defining what was meant by a "tendency to a breach of the peace", Avory J. said "What you have to ask yourself ... is whether these words ... are, in your opinion, indecent and offensive attacks on Christianity or the Scriptures or sacred persons or objects, calculated to outrage the feelings of the general body of the community and so lead, possibly - not inevitably, but so lead, possibly, to a breach of the peace. You must ask yourselves if a person of strong religious feelings had stopped to read this pamphlet whether his instinct might not have been to go up to the man who was selling it and give him a thrashing, or at all events, to use such language to him that a breach of the peace might be likely to be occasioned..." (p. 89).

66 Ibid., at p. 88.

17

several suggestions[67] that the law of blasphemy should be
invoked in regard to certain films which had been made
or were being planned, and in 1977, in the case of
Whitehouse v. Lemon and Gay News Ltd.[68] a private
prosecution was instituted. The editor and publisher of
a newspaper for homosexuals were indicted for blasphemous
libel for having published in an issue of the paper a poem
entitled "The Love that Dares to Speak its Name". The
poem recounted the homosexual fantasies of a Roman centurion
as he removed the body of Christ from the cross, in which
he described in explicit detail acts of sodomy and
fellatio with the body of Christ immediately after His
death and ascribed to Him during His lifetime promiscuous
homosexual practices with the Apostles and other men.[69]
We have already set out the substance of the trial judge's
definition of the constituent elements of blasphemy.[70] It
is further noteworthy that the trial judge quoted at length
from R. v. Gott,[71] and upon the basis of that case and
Bowman v. Secular Society Ltd.[72] directed the jury that the

---

67 A private prosecution in 1971 of the director of a play
    failed on a technicality. See also Tracey and Morrison,
    Whitehouse (1979), p. 113 and n. 362, below, for the
    attempt in 1972 to invoke the law of blasphemy against
    the BBC and pp. 4-5 as to the suggestion that it be
    invoked in the case of the plans by a Danish film-maker
    to make in Britain a film entitled The Many Faces of Jesus
    about the alleged sex life of Christ.

68 [1979] A.C. 617; also sub. nom. R. v. Lemon, R. v.
    Gay News Ltd., 11 July 1977 (Central Criminal Court,
    unrep.) and [1979] Q.B. 10 (C.A.). The prosecution
    was launched after legal advice indicated that a
    prosecution would have been less likely to succeed
    against earlier contemplated targets: Tracey and
    Morrison, op. cit., pp. 5-7.

69 See Whitehouse v. Lemon [1979] A.C. 617, 632, per
    Lord Diplock.

70 See para. 2.1, above.

71 (1922) 16 Cr. App. R. 87; see para. 2.14, above.

72 [1917] A.C. 406.

required element of a "tendency to cause a breach of the peace" means "to provoke or arouse angry feelings, something which is a possibility, not a probability". Upon this aspect of the case, he summarised the law to the jury in these terms: "The alleged blasphemy must be such as might well arouse anger or provoke strong feelings of resentment and be such that any reader could - not would but could - be provoked into committing a breach of the peace".[73] These parts of the direction were later repeated after the jury requested clarification of the meaning of "breach of the peace" and the "tendency" thereto.[74] The defendants were convicted on a majority verdict of 10 to 2.[75]

2.16 The principal ground of appeal attacked the trial judge's direction that the Crown did not have to prove an intent by the defendant to attack the Christian religion; "the relevant issue is ... must the defendants have had an intention to offend in the manner complained of, or is it enough that he or they intended to publish that which offends?"[76] In contending for the former the defence relied on R. v. Ramsay and Foote[77] and the approval therein of Starkie's view of the law.[78] The Court of Appeal rejected this contention:

> "intent in the sense for which the appellants have contended was not a live issue in Ramsay and Foote, for Foote, ... had admitted his intention .... Since this was the position

---

73 Transcript, p. 11a.

74 Ibid., p. 25.

75 Central Criminal Court, Judge King-Hamilton Q.C., 11 July 1977. A suspended sentence of 9 months on the editor was set aside by the Court of Appeal, [1979] Q.B. 10, 30, but fines of £500 and of £1000 on the company were upheld.

76 [1979] Q.B. 10, 16 (C.A.).

77 (1883) 15 Cox C.C. 231; para. 2.8, above.

78 See para. 2.7, above.

in that case, the passages in Starkie approved by Lord Coleridge cannot have been thought by [him] to have borne the meaning contended for by the appellants. The cases before Ramsay and Foote seem to us clearly to show that if an accused person deliberately published that which crossed the line which divided the blasphemous from the non-blasphemous, he could not be heard to say that he did not know or realise or intend that that which he had deliberately put into circulation possessed those characteristics which rendered him liable to conviction for blasphemy or blasphemous libel, according to whether the words in question were spoken or written".[79]

The Court of Appeal also rejected a second submission that the trial judge erred in ruling that the publication could be a blasphemous libel even though it did not "attack" the Christian religion. Although this word had been frequently used in reference to the offence,[80] "it was treated ... by the judges concerned as synonymous with that lack of due moderation and restraint which each jury concerned ... might think was appropriate having regard to the subject-matter under discussion."[81] The court relied on the repeated emphasis in Bowman's case[82] on the use of words such as "indecent", "offensive", "insulting", "ridicule", "vilification", "irreverence"; if the publication were "insulting" or "vilifying" and "the jury is prepared so to hold, then the law still today says, as it always has, that the publisher of such an attack, if vilifying or insulting, is guilty of blasphemous libel."[83]

---

79 [1979] Q.B. 10, 27.

80 See e.g. Bowman v. Secular Society Ltd. [1917] A.C. 406, 445, per Lord Parker of Waddington, quoted in para. 2.12, above.

81 R. v. Lemon [1979] Q.B. 10, 24.

82 See para. 2.12, above.

83 [1979] Q.B. 10, 24.

2.17   The Court of Appeal certified the following
question as being a point of law of general public
importance -

> "Was the learned trial judge correct first
> in ruling and then in directing the jury
> that in order to secure the conviction of
> the appellants for publishing a blasphemous
> libel
>
> (1) it was sufficient if the jury took the
>   view that the publication complained of
>   vilified Christ in His life and
>   crucifixion and
>
> (2) it was not necessary for the Crown to
>   establish any further intention on the
>   part of the appellants beyond an
>   intention to publish that which in the
>   jury's view was a blasphemous libel?"

By a majority of 3-2 the House of Lords[84] held that the
trial judge had been correct in ruling and directing the
jury in these terms; accordingly the appeal was dismissed.
The relatively narrow questions at issue in the case did
not afford the opportunity of a more general review of
tne law, although we refer below to some of the wide-
ranging observations of Lord Scarman in his speech.[85]

2.18   Of the majority, Viscount Dilhorne (with whose
analysis of the case law Lord Scarman agreed) referred
to the summing-up in R. v. Hetherington[86] as indicating
that at that date "it sufficed to show that what was published
was a blasphemous libel and that he [the publisher] was
responsible for its publication. This vicarious criminal
liability is wholly inconsistent with an intent to engage
in blasphemy being regarded at that time as an ingredient

---

84 [1979] A.C. 617, Viscount Dilhorne, Lord Russell and
    Lord Scarman (Lord Diplock and Lord Edmund-Davies
    dissenting).

85 See paras. 2.19, 3.1,6.4-6.6, 6.9, 7.20 and n. 352,
    below.

86 See para. 2.5, above.

of the offence."[87] In his view, the cases of R. v. Bradlaugh and R. v. Ramsay and Foote,[88] despite the explicit approval therein of the passage from Starkie which proclaimed the need for a "wilful intention to pervert, insult, and mislead others",[89] made no change in this respect. What these cases did do, according to Viscount Dilhorne, was to confirm that -

> "it is the manner in which they are expressed that may constitute views expressed in a publication a blasphemous libel and this passage from [Starkie] has been relied on as providing the test for determining whether the publication exceeds that which is permissible. It is the intention revealed by the publication that may lead to its being held to be blasphemous. There was nothing in Lord Coleridge's summing-up to support the view that there was a third question for the jury to consider, namely the intent of the accused."

In R. v. Ramsay and Foote Lord Coleridge -

> "cited the passage from Starkie, not as indicating that it must be shown that the accused had an intention to blaspheme but as providing the test for determining whether the articles exceeded the permissible bounds."[90]

Viscount Dilhorne concluded that the ingredients of the offence of publishing a blasphemous libel have not changed since Fox's Libel Act of 1792; it would in his view be surprising if they had, for if that which it is sought to prevent is the publication of blasphemous libels, "the harm is done by their intentional publication, whether or not the publisher intended to blaspheme."[91]

---

87   [1979] A.C. 617, 642-643.
88   See para. 2.8, above.
89   See para. 2.7, above.
90   [1979] A.C. 617, 644.
91   Ibid., p. 645.

2.19   Lord Scarman, who preceded his consideration of
the case with observations about the inadequacy, as he saw
it, of the common law offence,[92] said that the law had been
stated correctly by Lord Denman in R. v. Hetherington,[93]
and it had not been changed by Lord Coleridge's summing-up
in R. v. Ramsay and Foote.[94] "There was never any doubt,
or issue, in that case as to the accused's intention. Lord
Coleridge drew upon the passage in Professor Starkie's
famous work to explain not the mens rea but the nature of
the actus reus of blasphemy."[95] Lord Scarman expressly
held that the case law did not support Starkie's view,
quoted by Lord Coleridge, that a "wilful intention to
pervert, insult and mislead others ... is the criterion
and test of guilt." In his view, historically the law
required no more than an intention to publish words found
by the jury to be blasphemous. Even if a different view
were taken of historical developments, as a matter of
"legal policy in the society of today" Lord Scarman would
still have reached the same conclusion as to the elements
of blasphemous libel; for the law appeared to him -

> "to be moving towards a position in which
> people who know what they are doing will
> be criminally liable if the words they choose
> to publish are such as to cause grave offence
> to the religious feelings of some of their
> fellow citizens or are such as to tend to
> deprave and corrupt persons who are likely
> to read them."

Lord Scarman illustrated this "movement of the law" by
reference to the Obscene Publications Act 1959,

---

92   We refer to these observations below at paras. 6.9
     and 7.20.
93   See para. 2.5, above.
94   See para. 2.8, above.
95   [1979] A.C. 617, 664.

section 5A of the Public Order Act 1936,[96] and Articles 9 and 10 of the European Convention on Human Rights.[97] Article 9 of the Convention provides for freedom of religion and "by necessary implication" this "imposes a duty on all of us to refrain from insulting or outraging the religious feelings of others." Similarly, while Article 10 provides for freedom of expression, it also provides that the exercise of the freedom "carries with it duties and responsibilities" and may be restricted by law so far as necessary in a democratic society "for the prevention of disorder or crime, for the protection of health or morals, for the protection of the reputations or rights of others." Lord Scarman concluded that -

> "It would be intolerable if by allowing an author or publisher to plead the excellence of his motives and the right of free speech he could evade the penalties of the law even though his words were blasphemous in the sense of constituting an outrage upon the religious feelings of his fellow citizens. This is no way forward for a successful plural society. Accordingly, the test of obscenity by concentrating attention on the words complained of is, in my judgment, equally valuable as a test of blasphemy. The character of the words published matter; but not the motive of the author or publisher."[98]

2.20   In his short speech (with which Lord Scarman agreed), Lord Russell of Killowen pointed to the "apparently contradictory or ambivalent comments" in the authorities on the question before the House and refrained from analysing them. The House was "faced with a deliberate publication

---

96   See paras. 5.2 and 5.9, below; as explained in these paragraphs, neither offence requires a full mental element. See also paras. 6.4-6.5, below.

97   The Convention has been ratified by the United Kingdom and private citizens have the right of individual petition to the European Commission of Human Rights.

98   [1979] A.C. 617, 665; see further paras. 6.4-6.6, below.

of that which a jury with every justification has held
to be a blasphemous libel" and "the reason why the law
considers that the publication of a blasphemous libel
is an offence is that the law considers that such publication
should not take place." When a deliberate publication did
take place "I see no justification for holding that there
is no offence when the publisher is incapable for some
reason particular to himself of agreeing with a jury on
the true nature of the publication."[99]

2.21   Of the minority who would have allowed the appeal,
Lord Diplock, who agreed with Lord Edmund-Davies' analysis
of the case law, observed,[100] by contrast with both Viscount
Dilhorne and Lord Scarman, that the passage from Starkie
quoted by Lord Coleridge in R. v. Ramsay and Foote[101] -

> "clearly requires intent on the part of the
> accused himself to produce the described
> effect on those to whom the blasphemous
> matter is published and so removes blasphemous
> libel from the special category of offences in
> which mens rea as to at least one of the
> elements of the actus reus is not a necessary
> constituent element of the offence."

Furthermore, "significant changes" in the general concept
of mens rea in criminal law during the past hundred years
pointed to the propriety of adopting the view that the
offence required proof of "a 'specific intention', namely,
to shock and arouse resentment among those who believe in
or respect the Christian faith".[102] Among these changes
Lord Diplock pointed to the Criminal Evidence Act 1898,
which enabled a defendant to testify as a witness in his
own defence and so give direct evidence of his intention,

---

99 [1979] A.C. 617, 657-658.

100 [1979] A.C. 617, 635.

101 (1883) 15 Cox C.C. 231, 236; see paras. 2.7 and 2.8, above.

102 [1979] A.C. 617, 636.

and section 8 of the Criminal Justice Act 1967.[103] He admitted that these were relevant only if his view of the effect of Ramsay and Foote were accepted; but any other course would be -

> "a retrograde step which could not be justified by any considerations of public policy. The usual justification for creating by statute a criminal offence of strict liability, in which the prosecution need not prove mens rea as to one of the elements of the actus reus, is the threat that the actus reus of the offence poses to public health, public safety, public morals or public order. The very fact that there have been no prosecutions for blasphemous libel for more than fifty years is sufficient to dispose of any suggestion that in modern times a judicial decision to include this common law offence in this exceptional class of offences of strict liability could be justified upon grounds of public morals or public order."[104]

2.22   In his dissenting speech Lord Edmund-Davies paid particular attention to the effect of section 7 of the Libel Act 1843[105] and analysed at length the directions to the jury of Lord Coleridge C.J. in R. v. Bradlaugh[106] and R. v. Ramsay and Foote.[107] The summing-up in

---

103 This states that "a court or jury, in determining whether a person has committed an offence - (a) shall not be bound in law to infer that he intended or foresaw a result of his actions by reason only of its being a natural and probable consequence of those actions; but

(b) shall decide whether he did intend or foresee that result by reference to all the evidence, drawing such inferences from the evidence as appear proper in the circumstances". We have recommended repeal and replacement of the section by a wider provision in our Report on the Mental Element in Crime (1978) Law Com. No. 89, paras. 92-98. As to the importance of the Criminal Evidence Act 1898, see further para. 2.9, above.

104 [1979] A.C. 617, 638.

105 [1979] A.C. 617, 650 et seq; see para. 2.6, above.

106 (1883) 15 Cox C.C. 217; see para. 2.8, above.

107 (1883) 15 Cox C.C. 231; see para. 2.8, above.

R. v. Hetherington[108] was in his view of limited importance because at that date a defendant not only could not testify as to his intention, but was liable to be convicted "even if he lacked all knowledge that he had even published a blasphemy, and it would accordingly have been idle to investigate his intention in publishing." Since many cases of this period concerned publishing, the "publisher" rule restricted any judicial references there might have been to intention. Yet, even so, such references were to be found,[109] and Starkie, who was co-draftsman with Lord Campbell of the 1843 Act, had already set out his views[110] which were to be approved by Lord Coleridge. Lord Edmund-Davies concluded from his examination of Lord Coleridge's directions to the jury that, in regard to the question posed in each of the two cases as to whether the writings complained of were blasphemous libels, the proper answer "depended not merely on the words used but on the state of mind of the person using them".[111] As the Court of Appeal had noted,[112] the defendant Foote had admitted his intention. But this admitted intention was to attack Christianity; and Lord Coleridge considered that such an attack could not without more constitute the actus reus of blasphemy. The defendant had therefore not admitted an intent to blaspheme, as defined by Lord Coleridge. Thus "the intention of the defendants in publishing was assuredly a live issue in both trials, and Lord Coleridge made it clear that such was his view of the law."[113] Summarising, Lord Edmund-Davies considered that in the earliest stage blasphemy was a crime of strict liability,

---

108 (1841) 4 St. Tr. N.S. 563; see para. 2.5, above.

109 See para. 2.4, above.

110 See para. 2.7, above.

111 [1979] A.C. 617, 653.

112 [1979] Q.B. 10, 27; see para. 2.16, above.

113 [1979] A.C. 617, 653.

consisting merely of any attack upon the Christian church
and its tenets. In the second stage this harshness was
ameliorated, and the attack was not punishable unless
expressed in intemperate or scurrilous language. In the
third stage, some judges held that the subjective intention
of author or publisher was irrelevant, others that it was
of the greatest materiality. "The preponderance of
authority", he concluded "was nevertheless increasingly
and markedly in favour of the view that intention to
blaspheme must be established if conviction was to ensue.
In my judgment, such is now indeed the law."[114]

2.23   Before considering in more detail the elements
of the present law of blasphemous libel, we refer briefly
to statute law and past efforts at reform.

C. Statute Law

2.24   Until 1967 there was one statute, the Blasphemy
Act 1697, which created the offence of denying certain
tenets of the Christian religion after having been brought
up in or having professed that religion. There had been
few if any prosecutions under it, and in our Report on
Proposals to Abolish Certain Ancient Criminal Offences[115]
we took the view that it was obsolete and recommended that
it should be repealed. This recommendation was implemented
by the Criminal Law Act 1967.[116]

---

114   Ibid., p. 655.
115   (1966) Law Com. No. 3.
116   Sect. 13 and Sch. 4, Pt. 1. Certain ancient statutory
      offences of heresy and the like, contained in the
      Sacrament Act 1547, the Act of Supremacy 1558 and the
      Act of Uniformity 1662, have been repealed by the
      Statute Law (Repeals) Act 1969 and the Church of
      England (Worship and Doctrine) Measure 1974.

D.   Past attempts at law reform

2.25   For nearly a hundred years unsuccessful attempts
have been made to secure the abolition of the common law
offence. When Professor Kenny entered Parliament in 1885
he agreed to sponsor a "Religious Prosecutions Abolition
Bill" abolishing the common law and repealing the statutory
offence of blasphemy, but replacing them with a statutory
offence penalising intentional insults to religious
feelings.[117] In 1889 this was dropped in favour of
Bradlaugh's Bill drafted by Stephen, which would have
repealed and abolished all the laws relating to blasphemy
without any statutory saving of the kind contained in
Kenny's Bill. The Bill was, however, negatived on second
reading by 111 votes to 46. In 1914 Sir John Simon Q.C.,
then Attorney General, suggested reform of the law in an
opinion written for the Home Office[118] but no action was
taken. Bills similar to the Bradlaugh Bill were introduced
in 1923 and 1925, but reached the stage of debate only in
1930 when a Blasphemy Laws (Amendment) Bill was approved
after debate by 131 votes to 77.[119] This was drastically
altered in Standing Committee by a Government amendment
which sought to introduce a statutory offence of outraging
religious convictions;[120] its sponsors thereupon dropped
it. In 1966 a sub-committee of the Criminal Law Revision
Committee, which was then considering the abolition of all
common law misdemeanours, concluded that blasphemy should
be abolished without replacement, but no further progress

---

117   Modelled on the Indian Penal Code; see para. 4.10,
      below and generally Kenny, "The Evolution of the Law
      of Blasphemy" (1922) 1 Cambridge L.J. 127 at p. 138.
      As to the draft Code of 1879, see n. 28, above.

118   See Blom-Cooper and Drewry (eds.), Law and Morality:
      A Reader (1976), p. 252.

119   Hansard, H.C. (1930) Vol. 234, col. 572.

120   See further para. 8.3, below.

was made. The Blasphemy (Abolition of Offence) Bill,
introduced in the House of Lords in January 1978, provided
for the abolition of the common law offences of blasphemy,
profanity, and blasphemous or profane libels, but, after
a debate[121] in which it was announced that the Law
Commission was to examine the law, and in which a wide
range of opinion was expressed, the Bill failed to get a
second reading.[122]

III THE PRESENT LAW

A. The prohibited conduct (actus reus)

1. Insult, vilification and "attack"

3.1   According to the definition in Stephen's Digest[123]
approved by Lord Scarman in Whitehouse v. Lemon[124] any
publication is blasphemous "which contains any contemptuous,
reviling, scurrilous or ludicrous matter relating to God,
Jesus Christ, or the Bible, or the formularies of the
Church of England as by the law established." We have
noted that, save in regard to the possible requirement of
a tendency to lead to a breach of the peace, the trial
judge's definition of the elements of the offence, upon
which neither the Court of Appeal nor any member of the
House of Lords commented adversely,[125] was substantially
the same. In the light of the authorities, particularly
Bowman v. Secular Society Ltd.,[126] it is probable that

---

121   Hansard, H.L. (1978) Vol. 389, cols. 279-350; see
      further, paras. 7.7 and 7.12, below.

122   Ibid., at Col. 350.

123   (9th ed., 1950) Art. 214; see further para. 2.1,
      above.

124   [1979] A.C. 617, 665-666.

125   See para. 2.1, above.

126   [1917] A.C. 406; see para. 2.12, above; and see
      Whitehouse v. Lemon [1979] Q.B. 10, 24, and para. 2.16,
      above.

emphasis must lie on the "reviling" or "scurrilous" nature
of the material, rather than its "contemptuous" or "ludicrous"
character. Lord Scarman also referred to blasphemy's
"efficacy to protect religious feelings from outrage and
insult" and to words which are "blasphemous in the sense
of constituting an outrage upon the religious feelings of
[an author's or publisher's] fellow citizens";[127] but these
were in the nature of observations upon the functions of
the law and the alleged effect of the offending conduct
and did not form part of the definition which he approved.
Furthermore, it is settled that an "attack" on the Christian
religions is not an essential element of the offence: an
attack may be couched in terms which do not insult or vilify
and, if this is the case, the law does not penalise it.
But if the words are an outrage upon the feelings of the
"general body of the community", the opinion or argument
they are used to advance or destroy is "of no moment".[128]
On the other hand, in considering whether the words
complained of went beyond "permitted limits", there is some
authority for the view that the place and circumstances of
publication may be taken into account.[129]

---

127 See [1979] A.C. 617, 658 and 665.

128 Whitehouse v. Lemon [1979] A.C. 617, 662 per Lord
Scarman. See also the remarks of the Court of Appeal
[1979] Q.B. 10, 17, quoted in para. 2.16, above.

129 R. v. Boulter (1908) 72 J.P. 188: "when we come to
consider whether he has exceeded the permitted limits,
we must not neglect to consider the place where he
speaks and the people to whom he speaks. A man is
not free in a public place, where passers-by who
might not willingly go to listen to him knowing what
he was going to say, might accidentally hear his words,
or where young people might be present - a man is not
free in such places to use coarse ridicule on subjects
which are sacred to most people in this country. He
is free to advance argument" (per Phillimore J., at
p. 189).

3.2   It seems that the Christian religion in general
is protected, together with the doctrines and rituals of the
Church of England but not those of other religions or other
Christian bodies.   In 1838 Alderson B. stated in a direction
to a jury in a case of criminal libel[130] that -

> "a person may, without being liable to
> prosecution for it, attack Judaism, or
> Mahomedanism, or even any sect of the
> Christian religion (save the established
> religion of the country); and the only
> reason why the latter is in a different
> situation from the others is, because it
> is the form established by law, and is
> therefore a part of the constitution of
> the country. In like manner, and for the
> same reason, any general attack on
> Christianity is the subject of a criminal
> prosecution, because Christianity is the
> established religion of the country".

This was, however, thought to be a "strange dictum" by
Lord Sumner in Bowman v. Secular Society Ltd.,[131] since
"after all, to insult a Jew's religion is not less likely
to provoke a fight than to insult an episcopalian's".
The Canadian courts, as we note below,[132] have followed
a different course. Whatever the scope of the offence in
England and Wales, Lord Scarman clearly took the view that
protection under the present law does not extend beyond
the Christian religion.[133]

---

130 R. v. Gathercole (1838) 2 Lew. C.C. 237, 254; 168 E.R.
     1140, 1145, in which the defendant was found guilty of
     criminal libel for publishing an attack on a Roman
     Catholic nunnery.

131 [1917] A.C. 406, 460.

132 See para. 4.7, below.

133 [1979] A.C. 617, 658; see further para. 6.9, below, and
     Nokes, A History of the Crime of Blasphemy (1928) pp.
     102-117. It should be noted that the Church in Wales
     was disestablished in 1920 (see Welsh Church Act 1914,
     s. 1 and the Welsh Church (Temporalities) Act 1919, s.2);
     thus it is not "the form established by law" nor "part
     of the constitution" of the Principality (see R. v.
     Gathercole above). There is no authority as to whether
     this has had any effect upon the operation of the law
     of blasphemy in Wales.

2. Tendency to lead to a breach of the peace

3.3   We have noted that in the 18th and early 19th
centuries blasphemy was penalised because of its "supposed
tendency in fact to shake the fabric of society"[134] in
the sense of severe civil disturbance. But by the early
20th century blasphemy no longer had any such effect[135]
and for that reason the offence was pronounced a "dead
letter" by Lord Denning in 1949.[136] However, a tendency
to cause a breach of the peace, in its narrow sense of any
disturbance to the peace, was specified as an element of
the offence by Lord Parker in Bowman v. Secular Society
Ltd.[137] and emphasised by Avory J. in R. v. Gott.[138] From
that case it seemed that, while there was no need for any
evidence of an actual breach of the peace, it had to be
proved that, in consequence of the publication in question,
there was a likelihood of a breach of the peace.[139] This
requirement was further diluted by the trial judge in R. v.
Lemon, who in his summing-up said that a tendency to cause
a breach of the peace means "to provoke or arouse angry
feelings, something which is a possibility, not a
probability".[140] The trial judge also ruled that it is
unnecessary to prove a subjective intent to cause a breach

---

134   Bowman v. Secular Society Ltd. [1917] A.C. 406, 459
       per Lord Sumner; see paras. 2.2 and 2.13, above.

135   Ibid., at p. 467; see para. 2.13, above.

136   See para. 2.13, above.

137   [1917] A.C. 406, 445-446; see paras. 2.12-2.13, above.

138   (1922) 16 Cr. App. R. 87, 88; see para. 2.14, above.

139   Ibid., see n. 65, above.

140   Transcript, p. 11a; see para. 2.15, above. It is
       noteworthy that between Gott and Lemon the Court of
       Criminal Appeal held that, in the law of criminal
       libel (see para. 5.1, below), it is not necessary
       to prove that the libel in question was likely to
       result in a breach of the peace: R. v. Wicks (1936)
       25 Cr. App. R. 168; approved in Gleaves v. Deakin
       [1980] A.C. 477.

of the peace.[141] Even the vestigial requirement of a
tendency to cause a breach of the peace retained by the
trial judge was, it seems, altogether eliminated by Lord
Scarman in Whitehouse v. Lemon, when he stated that the
phrase is really a reference to the true test of "whether
the words are calculated to outrage and insult the
Christian's religious feelings".[142] As we have noted,[143]
this "true test" is itself more in the nature of a comment
upon the alleged effect of the conduct penalised than part
of the definition of the offence approved by Lord Scarman.

3.4   It will be evident that it is now uncertain
whether a tendency to lead to a breach of the peace is an
essential element of the offence. According to the trial
judge in Lemon, there is such a requirement, albeit
vestigial in character; in Lord Scarman's view not even
this vestigial requirement survives. But even if it does,
the meaning of a "tendency to a breach of the peace" as
elucidated by the trial judge is not consistent with its
meaning elsewhere in the criminal law. In particular, it
is noteworthy that in the context of the duty of a
constable to prevent breaches of the peace which he

---

141 This was approved by the Court of Appeal: see [1979]
     Q.B. 10, 17. But in the House of Lords, Lord
     Edmund-Davies, purporting in this respect to agree
     with the Court of Appeal, said that there was no need
     for "the publication, when objectively considered, [to]
     tend to lead to a breach of the peace" ([1979] A.C. 617,
     656; emphasis added). With respect, we suggest that, if
     this was meant to accord with the views of the trial
     judge and the Court of Appeal, Lord Edmund-Davies must
     have intended the word "subjectively".

142 [1979] A.C. 617, 662. Lord Scarman further commented
     that "the use of the phrase is no more than a minor
     contribution to the discussion of the subject. It
     does remind us that we are in the field where the
     law seeks to safeguard public order and tranquillity"
     (ibid., p. 662); see para. 5.8 and n. 223, below.

143 See para. 3.1, above.

34

reasonably apprehends, it seems that the duty to take such steps as he reasonably thinks are necessary only arises if proved facts existed from which he could reasonably have anticipated a breach of the peace as a "real", as distinct from a "remote" or "mere" possibility, and he did so anticipate.[144] We refer again to this aspect of the actus reus below in discussing the defects of the law.[145]

3. Publication

(a) In general

3.5   Publication may be oral or written; if the former, the offence is blasphemy, if the latter, blasphemous libel. As we mention elsewhere, no mental element is required other than the intent to publish, and no proof is needed that the statement in question caused a breach of the peace. It seems to follow that publication to one other person is sufficient to satisfy this element of the offence, although there appears to have been no prosecution in these circumstances. There is no authority on the question whether statements made on television or in other broadcasts may be the subject of proceedings for blasphemy or blasphemous libel. Although sections 1 and 16(3) of the Defamation Act 1952 provide in regard to civil proceedings that the broadcasting of "words"[146] for general reception by wireless telegraphy should be treated as publication in permanent form, that is, as libel, by section 17(2) the Act does not apply to criminal libel; thus it is

---

144   Piddington v. Bates [1961] 1 W.L.R. 162, 169. See Smith and Hogan, Criminal Law (4th ed., 1978) p. 363; but see further R. v. Podger [1979] Crim. L.R. 524, and also comment on the case of R. v. Ratiu in (1979) 129 New L.J. 943.

145   See para. 6.2, below.

146   Defined by s. 16(1) to include "pictures, visual images, gestures and other methods of signifying meaning".

of doubtful assistance in assessing the position in regard
to criminal forms of libel generally. In principle,
however, there seems to be no reason why statements or
visual images which are published by means of radio or
television transmissions should not be liable to criminal
proceedings for blasphemous libel at common law.[147] In
the case of written statements, there are various statutory
provisions relating to publication of blasphemous material
which require more detailed consideration.

(b)   The Libel Act 1843

3.6   Section 7 of the Libel Act 1843 provides that,
when a defendant pleads not guilty to the publication of
a libel, evidence which establishes a "presumptive case"
of publication against him "by the act of any other person
by his authority" may be rebutted by him on proof of
evidence "that such publication was made without his
authority, consent or knowledge, and that the said
publication did not arise from want of due care or
caution on his part." This provision applies to
blasphemous as well as defamatory libel. Thus a person who
allows publication of a paper on his premises and is aware
of its general character may nonetheless not be guilty of
publishing blasphemous libels if he is otherwise
unconnected with the paper at the relevant time, even
though it is published by someone employed by him.[148] Where
presumptive evidence of editorship is given, the fact
that there is no direct evidence that the editor was
personally responsible for publishing the blasphemous libel

---

147   As to statutory provisions relevant in this context
      to broadcasting, see para. 5.13, below.

148   R. v. Bradlaugh (1883) 15 Cox C.C. 217, following
      R. v. Holbrook (1878) 4 Q.B.D. 42 (a case of criminal
      libel), and approved by Lord Edmund-Davies in Whitehouse
      v. Lemon [1979] A.C. 617, 650 (diss.): see para. 2.22,
      above.

will not suffice to displace that presumptive evidence, and the editor will be guilty.[149]

(c) The Law of Libel Amendment Act 1888

3.7   Two provisions of the Law of Libel Amendment Act 1888 are of particular relevance in the context of blasphemy. By section 3 -

> "A fair and accurate report in any newspaper of proceedings publicly heard before any court exercising judicial authority shall, if published contemporaneously with such proceedings, be privileged; provided nothing in this section shall authorise the publication of any blasphemous or indecent matter."

By section 8 -

> "no criminal prosecution shall be commenced against any proprietor, publisher, editor or any person responsible for the publication of a newspaper for any libel published therein without the order of a Judge at Chambers being first had and obtained. Such application shall be made on notice to the person accused, who shall have an opportunity of being heard against such application."[150]

This was the course adopted in Whitehouse v. Lemon. In Goldsmith v. Pressdram Ltd.,[151] Wien J. referred to three matters which had to be satisfied before he would exercise

---

149   R. v. Lemon [1979] Q.B. 10, 29 (C.A.).

150   This section was inserted at the instance of Lord Coleridge C.J., who was incensed at the frequency with which the Director of Public Prosecutions gave his fiat for prosecution of newspapers under the Newspaper Libel and Registration Act 1881: see Spencer, "The Press and the Reform of Criminal Libel" in Glazebrook (ed.), Reshaping the Criminal Law (1978) pp. 277 et seq.

151   [1977] Q.B. 83, 88. Sect. 8 is to be considered in more detail in the context of our work on criminal libel: see para. 1.3, above.

his discretion to order a prosecution for criminal libel. First, there had to be a prima facie case. Secondly, the libel had to be so serious that it was proper for the criminal law to be invoked; it might be relevant, but not necessary, that it was unusually likely for it to provoke a breach of the peace. Thirdly, the public interest should require institution of criminal proceedings. These considerations are presumably applicable to all types of libel subject to the criminal law, including blasphemous libel.

B. The mental element (mens rea)

3.8   We have noted that both the Court of Appeal and the House of Lords in _Whitehouse_ v. _Lemon_ affirmed that, while the defendant must intend to publish, he need not intend that the words should amount to a blasphemous publication.[152]   It follows, as the Court of Appeal and the House of Lords also pointed out[153] that no admissible evidence can be given by the publisher or the author as to their respective intentions in publishing and writing the alleged blasphemy. Still less is there any opportunity (such as is offered by the defence of public good in section 4 of the Obscene Publications Act 1959 in the context of obscene publications)[154] to give evidence, for example, as to the theological or other implications of the article in support of any alleged intent of the author or publisher. The Court of Appeal also affirmed the correctness of the trial judge's direction to the jury that it was not an essential ingredient of blasphemy that there should have been a subjective intention on the part of the defendant

---

152   [1979] Q.B. 10, 27; [1979] A.C. 617, 645 (Viscount Dilhorne), 657-658 (Lord Russell), 664 and 665 (Lord Scarman); see paras. 2.16-2.20, above.

153   _Ibid_., at pp.16 and 27-28, and [1979] A.C. 617, at pp. 657 (Lord Russell) and 665 (Lord Scarman).

154   See para. 5.2, below.

to provoke a breach of the peace.[155]

C. Procedure and penalty

3.9   No consent to institution of proceedings is
required; thus any member of the public may institute
proceedings for blasphemy or blasphemous libel. We have,
however, noted above the special procedure which applies
when the defendant is a newspaper editor, publisher or
proprietor. The offences are triable only on indictment
and are punishable with a fine and imprisonment, upon which
there are no statutory limits.[156] In addition, section 1
of the Criminal Libel Act 1819 enables a court in which a
judgment or verdict has been obtained against a defendant
for the composition, printing or publishing of any
blasphemous (or seditious) libel to order the confiscation
of all copies of the libel in the possession of the
defendant or of anyone else shown by evidence on oath to
possess it for the use of the defendant. Under the order
a Justice of the Peace or constable or persons acting under
their authority are empowered to search for copies of the
libel and, by day, to enter premises by force should
admission be refused.

IV BLASPHEMY IN OTHER LEGAL SYSTEMS

4.1   Before considering the defects of the present law
of England and Wales, we survey the way in which blasphemy
is treated in other jurisdictions, both at common law and in
civil law systems.

---

155 [1979] Q.B. 10, 17; see para. 3.3 and n.141, above.
156 See para. 3.7, above; and see further, notes 64 and 75,
     above.

A. Scotland

4.2   Blasphemy is an offence at common law in Scotland committed by the uttering of impious and profane things against God or the authority of the Holy Scriptures when it is done in a "scoffing or railing manner, out of a reproachful disposition in the speaker, and ... with passion against the Almighty, rather than with any purpose of propagating the irreverent opinion".[157] Although there have been no cases concerning the spoken word for several centuries, it is probable that the crime covers both written and verbal utterances. The most recent judicial dictum concerning the law in Scotland appears to be in Bowman v. Secular Society Ltd. where Lord Finlay L.C. said that in Scotland, as in England, "the crime of blasphemy is not constituted by a temperate attack on religion in which the decencies of controversy are maintained".[158] But the offence has played such a small part in Scottish legal history that it has been doubted whether it now exists.[159] Two points may however be made with some certainty. First, the last reported convictions for blasphemy date from the 1840's, following several prosecutions of booksellers and publishers in Edinburgh for publishing and selling books of an anti-religious, politically radical or obscene nature.[160]

---

157   Hume, Commentaries on the Law of Scotland Respecting Crimes (4th ed., 1844) Vol.II, p. 568.

158   [1917] A.C. 406, 423; see also Lord Dunedin at pp.433-434.

159   Gordon, Criminal Law (2nd ed., 1978) pp.998, who states that "it may be said that blasphemy is no longer a crime".

160   Henry Robinson (1843) 1 Brown. 590, 643; Thomas Paterson ibid., p. 629; Thomas Finlay, ibid., p. 648 n.

It is noteworthy that the Lord Justice Clerk (Hope) in his charge to the jury said the prosecutions were justified because the activities of the accused were likely, and probably intended, to lead to public disorder or at least to breach of the peace. Secondly, "the existence of the common law crime is theoretical only, for the simple reason that the Crown[161] is unlikely to initiate any prosecution for blasphemy as such and will prefer some other charge instead.... Today any alleged blasphemous conduct would be dealt with as obscenity or breach of the peace".[162]

B. Ireland

4.3   The position in the Republic of Ireland is complicated by the provisions of its constitution. At the beginning of this century, the few Irish cases appeared to establish that, by contrast with the position in England, the common law offence of blasphemy might be committed because of the matter rather than the manner of what was said or done.[163] Whether the Irish common law was modified

---

161 Private prosecutions such as occurred in Whitehouse v. Lemon are virtually impossible to bring in Scotland since a private prosecutor has to indicate some special personal interest rather than merely being one of an offended public. In Meehan v. Inglis and others 1974 S.L.T. 61 (Notes), the court said: "The court has the ultimate say on whether a private prosecution should be granted, even when the Lord Advocate has refused his concurrence, but ... it would require some very special circumstances indeed to induce the court to make an exception to what has now become a settled practice" [i.e. that the decision to sanction a prosecution lies with the Lord Advocate].

162 Maher, "Blasphemy in Scots Law" 1977 Scots L.T. 257 at p. 260.

163 See O'Higgins, "Blasphemy in Irish Law" (1960) 23 M.L.R. 151, especially pp. 161-166.

as a result of the House of Lords' decision in Bowman v.
Secular Society Ltd.[164] is uncertain. The Constitution
of the Republic now qualifies the constitutional guarantee
of the right of citizens to express freely their
convictions and opinions with the proviso that -

> "The publication or utterance of blasphemous,
> seditious or indecent matter is an offence
> which shall be unishable in accordance
> with law".[165]

There is, so far as we are aware, no case law to indicate
the meaning of "blasphemous", in particular whether this
provision altered the pre-existing common law. But there
is support for the view that the Constitution created no
new offence, and that blasphemy is an offence at common
law.[166]

4.4   There have also been no recent cases in Northern
Ireland, and it is uncertain whether the common law there
would now reflect developments in the common law of England
and Wales resulting from Bowman and Lemon.[167]

C.   Other common law systems

1.   General

4.5   With some exceptions, states whose criminal law
has its roots in the common law still penalise blasphemy,

---

164 [1917] A.C. 406.
165 Art. 40.6.I.i.
166 See O'Higgins, op. cit., p. 160.
167 As to the Prevention of Incitement to Hatred Act
     (Northern Ireland) 1970, see para. 5.12, below.

either at common law or by specific statutory or codified provisions. However, since these states have no established Church, the law there differs from the common law of England and Wales, which, as we have seen, apparently protects only the Church of England.[168] New Zealand and Canada[169] have provisions in their Codes, based on the English Draft Code of 1879.[170] In the U.S.A. blasphemy is penalised as a common law misdemeanour and in addition by legislation in many states,[171] although no provision for it is made in the American Law Institute's Model Penal Code of 1962. The Indian Penal Code contains special provisions which differ radically from the offence of blasphemy at common law.[172] In Australia, those states which do not have criminal codes[173] retain the common law offence of blasphemous libel, although there is little, if any, authority on it from cases decided in those jurisdictions. On the other hand, the Queensland Criminal Code, even though based largely on the English Draft Code of 1879, makes no provision for blasphemy,[174] and recent proposals for criminal codes in those states whose criminal law is

---

168   See para. 3.2, above.

169   See para. 4.7 and n. 182, below.

170   See n. 28, above.

171   See further, paras. 4.8-4.9, below.

172   See paras. 4.10-4.11, below.

173   New South Wales, Victoria and South Australia, the Northern Territory and Australian Capital Territory (and the Commonwealth within the scope of its constitutional powers).

174   But under the Objectionable Literature Acts 1954-1967 the Literature Board of Review may prevent distribution of "objectionable" literature; and "objectionable" is very widely defined to include blasphemy, obscenity and incitement to public disorder and crime.

still uncodified also omit it. In particular, in its Report on the Substantive Criminal Law, the Criminal Law and Penal Methods Reform Committee of South Australia commented that "today it would seem anachronistic to charge anyone with blasphemous libel" and recommended that criminal libel (which it described as including blasphemous or seditious libels, libels affecting the administration of justice and other defamatory libels) "should not be retained except for libels in relation to affairs of State and the administration of justice".[175]

4.6   It is worth examining in more detail some contrasting treatments of the law in countries where the common law is in force or remains influential. For this purpose we have selected Canada, the United States and India.

2.   Canada

4.7   Section 260 of the Canadian Criminal Code provides that -

> "(1) Everyone who publishes a blasphemous libel is guilty of an indictable offence and is liable to imprisonment for two years.
>
> (2) It is a question of fact whether or not any matter that is published is a blasphemous libel.
>
> (3) No person shall be convicted of an offence under this section for expressing in good faith and in decent language, or

---

175 Report on the Substantive Criminal Law (1977), pp. 248-249. The Draft Criminal Code for the Australian Territories likewise makes no provision for blasphemy or blasphemous libel; see Parliamentary Papers of the Commonwealth of Australia, 1969, No. 44.

attempting to establish by argument
used in good faith and conveyed in
decent language, an opinion upon a
religious subject".

In R. v. Kinler[176] it was held that only a direct attack on
the Deity would now be regarded as blasphemous libel, and
that neither an attack on the clergy nor on the doctrine of
a particular Church would constitute the offence. But in
R. v. St. Martin[177] the defendant, a man of wide knowledge,
was convicted for the publication of articles in which he
caustically attacked the Roman Catholic faith and Christian
virtues and the various religious practices of the majority
of the people of Quebec. This was cited in R. v. Rahard[178]
where the defendant, an Anglican priest who published matter
offensive to Roman Catholics on posters affixed to his
church property in Montreal, Quebec, was convicted of
blasphemous libel. The court referred to the English
authorities as to what constituted a blasphemous libel,[179]
but made no reference to the authorities in English law
which suggest that protection is confined to Christianity

---

176 (1925) 63 Que. S.C. 483.

177 (1933) 40 Rev. de Jur. 411.

178 [1936] 3 D.L.R. 230 (Court of Sessions of the Peace,
     Quebec, 1935).

179 At that time, the view was held that "the common law
     jurisdiction as to crime is still operative
     notwithstanding the Criminal Code, but subject
     to the latter prevailing where there is a
     repugnancy between the common law and the Code":
     R. v. Cole (1902) 5 Can. C.C. 330. The Code
     now provides in s. 7(2) that the English criminal
     law in force in a province before 1 April 1955
     continues in force save as altered, varied,
     modified or affected by the Code or any
     other Act of the Canadian Parliament.

and the Church of England.[180] It concluded that the
publication did not fall within subsection (3) above
because there was no argument in it "expressed in good faith
or decent language"; on the contrary, the publication was
blasphemous as its terms were "offensive and injurious to
the Roman Catholics and of such a nature that they may lead
to a disturbance of the public peace" and the language used
was "calculated and intended to insult the feelings and the
deepest religious convictions of the great majority of the
persons amongst whom we live".[181] Thus it seems that the
provisions of the Canadian Criminal Code extend to the
Christian religion generally but not beyond it.[182]

3.   The United States of America

4.8   According to a leading textbook, since there is
no established church as in England, no act is a crime in
the United States merely because it offends against any
church, or against God, or against religious doctrines;
but blasphemy is one of a number of activities which, if
committed under such circumstances as to constitute a
public nuisance, are indictable as common law misdemeanours.
This is because they annoy the community or shock its sense

---

180   See para. 3.2, above.

181   R. v. Rahard, ibid., at pp. 237-238; the last
      quotation adopts the summing-up of Coleridge L.C.J. in
      R. v. Bradlaugh (1883) 15 Cox C.C. 217, 230: see para.
      2.8, above.

182   The New Zealand Crimes Act 1961 s. 123 is in terms
      similar to the Canadian Code, save that the maximum
      term of imprisonment is one year, and prosecution
      requires leave of the Attorney General. In regard to
      the law in New Zealand it has been stated that "it
      is doubtful whether it can be said that the Christian
      religion is part of New Zealand common law, and, if it
      is not, the main reason for giving preference to the
      Christian faith disappears": Adams, Criminal Law and
      Practice in New Zealand (2nd ed., 1971) p. 258. There
      have been no reported prosecutions for blasphemous
      libel in New Zealand since 1922.

of morality and decency or have a tendency to disturb the public peace.[183] Whatever may be the basis for the offence, its content[184] appears not to differ greatly from English common law as it was understood to be in the early 19th century. The offence consists in "maliciously reviling God or religion" and may be classified under three heads "(1) denying the being and providence of God; (2) contumelious reproaches of Jesus Christ; profane and malevolent scoffing of the Scriptures, or exposing any part of them to contempt and ridicule; (3) certain immoralities tending to subvert all religion and morality, which are the foundations of all governments". But "a wilful and malicious intent in assailing God or the doctrine of the Christian religion is necessary to render a person guilty of blasphemy".[185]

4.9   In many State jurisdictions statutes have been enacted defining blasphemy and prescribing the punishment. Even though a criminal statute may be held unconstitutional because it is intended to promote a particular kind of religion,[186] the constitutionality of these statutes has been generally upheld against the claim that they violated constitutional guarantees of freedom of speech of the

---

183   Clarke and Marshall, A Treatise on the Law of Crimes (7th ed., 1967) p. 96.

184   See Wharton's Criminal Law and Procedure (1957) Vol.II, pp. 666-669.

185   Quotations from Wharton, pp. 666-668, based on the authority of early cases.

186   By the 1st Amendment, "Congress shall make no law ... prohibiting the free exercise" of religion and no law "respecting an establishment of religion". Thus in Epperson v. Arkansas (1968) 393 U.S.97, 89 S. Cr. 266, a statute making it a misdemeanour to teach the theory of evolution in public schools was held unconstitutional. See Lafave and Scott, Handbook on the Criminal Law (1972) p. 158.

press or of religious liberty or worship.[187]

4. India

4.10   Section 298 of the Indian Penal Code provides
that -

> "Whoever, with the deliberate intention of
> wounding the religious feelings of any person,
> utters any word or makes any sound in the
> hearing of that person or makes any gesture
> in the sight of that person, or places any
> object in the sight of that person, shall be
> punished with imprisonment ... for a term
> which may extend to one year, or with
> fine or with both".

The background to this provision is noteworthy.
Lord Macaulay said in a Parliamentary speech in 1833 that
"It is monstrous to see any Judge try a man for blasphemy
under the present law", but added "no man ought to be at
liberty to force, upon unwilling ears and eyes, sounds and
sights which must cause irritation.... If I were a Judge
in India, I should have no scruple about punishing a
Christian who should pollute a mosque". Hence the above
section embodied in the draft Code of 1837 drawn up by the
first Indian Law Commission of which he was President;[188]

---

187 Wharton's Criminal Law and Procedure (1957)
     Vol. II, p. 669.

188 See Kenny "The Evolution of the Law of Blasphemy"
     (1922) 1 C.L.J. at p. 135. Some of the Codes adopting
     the Indian model have the same or a similar provision
     e.g., s. 298 of the Malaysian Penal Code. Others have
     adopted a different approach e.g., s. 210 of the
     Northern Nigerian Penal Code penalises "whoever by any
     means publicly insults or seeks to incite contempt for
     any religion in such a manner as to be likely to lead
     to a breach of the peace...."

the draft Code was subsequently revised and completed in
1850, although it did not come into force until 1861. In
their observations upon what is now section 298, the
Indian Law Commission commented that, under the section,
there had to be a deliberate and premeditated intention to
wound: words uttered in good faith in the heat of an
argument were not covered. And a leading commentator points
out that while "deliberate intention of the accused may be
inferred from his words as well as from his acts, ... [a]
mere knowledge of the likelihood that the religious feelings
of other persons may be wounded would not suffice nor a mere
intention to wound such feelings ... unless that intention
was deliberate".[189]

4.11   It is noteworthy that section 298 does not
penalise the intention to wound religious feelings by means
of written matter. This is covered by section 295A,
inserted in the Code in 1927, which provides -

> "Whoever, with the deliberate and malicious
> intention of outraging the religious feelings
> of any class of citizens of India, by words, either
> spoken or written, or [by signs or] by visible
> representations [or otherwise] insults or
> attempts to insult the religion or the religious
> beliefs of that class, shall be punished with
> imprisonment ... for a term which may extend to
> three years, or with fine, or with both" (the
> bracketed words were added in 1961).

---

189 See Ranchhoddas and Thakore, The Law of Crimes (21st
     ed., 1966) pp. 720-721 and Chitaley and Rao, Indian
     Penal Code (2nd ed., 1974) Vol.2, pp. 753-756. The
     case-law cited in the former indicates that for the
     most part it is only where there are clear and serious
     breaches that charges under s. 298 will successfully
     be brought. Thus it has been held an offence for a
     Muslim to garland and parade a cow before sacrificing
     it in a public place and thereafter to carry the
     carcass in a cot, with horns and legs protruding,
     on a public way (Gulab [1955] Cr.L.J. 168); or to kill
     a cow in the presence of Hindus (Mir Chittan [1936]
     A.L.J.R. 1197) or to exhibit cows flesh by carrying
     it in an uncovered state round a village with the
     deliberate intent of wounding the religious feelings of
     Hindus (Rahman (1893) 13 A.W.N. 144).

Apart from its specific application to written matter, this provision differs from section 298 in requiring, first, a deliberate "and malicious" intention. It seems that the reference to "malice" was inserted to exclude from liability the writer whose object is to facilitate social reform by shocking the followers of a religion into taking note of his criticisms; but "in almost all cases [malice] has to be inferred from surrounding circumstances having regard to the setting, background and connected facts in relation to the editing and publishing of the offending article".[190] Secondly, the section requires an intent to "outrage" rather than to "wound"; outrage is regarded as a much stronger word.[191] Thirdly, there must be an "insult" or "attempt to insult" religion or religious beliefs: manner rather than matter has to be considered.[192]

D. Civil law codes

4.12   There is no observable consistency in treatment of blasphemy in European civil law codes. For example, the French Penal Code contains nothing pertaining to such conduct.[193] On the other hand, section 166 of the German

---

190 Ranchhoddas and Thakore, ibid., p. 712; and see Chitaley and Rao, ibid., pp. 739-745.

191 Ranchhoddas and Thakore, ibid., p. 712.

192 Ibid., pp. 711-712.

193 Although Art. 283 penalises making and publishing matter which is immoral ("contraire aux bonnes moeurs") and Art. 284 the publicising of debauchery and other "immoral utterances".

Penal Code penalises anyone who, in public, or by publishing written, recorded or pictorial material or representations, insults in a way liable to disturb the public peace either (a) religious or philosophical beliefs or (b) any Church in the country or other religious or philosophical society,[194] or their institutions or traditions. The Netherlands Criminal Code also contains comprehensive provisions penalising blasphemous conduct,[195] although we understand that there has been only one successful prosecution in the last forty years. Again, the Swedish Penal Code contains nothing about blasphemy,[196] whereas section 142 of the Norwegian code penalises anybody who, by word or deed, publicly insults or in an offensive or injurious way shows disdain for a religious creed permitted in Norway, or for the dogma or worship of any religious community lawfully existing there. The Greek code, by Articles 198-199, penalises those who publicly and maliciously by any means blaspheme God and the Greek Orthodox Church or any other religion permitted in Greece. The emphasis in Article 173 of the Turkish code is upon violation of religious services, although it provides in addition penalties on anyone who makes a publication to humiliate or debase any religions or sects. Finally, it is noteworthy that Article 193 of the Polish People's Republic Penal Code penalises anyone who in public insults, derides, humiliates or commits an assault on others on account either of their not having a religious affiliation or on account of their religious affiliation; while

---

194   i.e. "Weltanschauungsvereinigung".

195   Articles 147, 147a and 429 bis.

196   Although s.7 penalises a person who publicly threatens or expresses contempt for a group of a certain race, skin colour, national or ethnic origin or religious creed.

51

Article 198 penalises anyone who offends the religious
feelings of others by outraging in public an object of
religious worship or a place dedicated to the public
celebration of religious rites.

E. Conclusions

4.13   This survey of other legal systems leads to no
obvious conclusions of immediate assistance in suggesting
the way forward for changes in the law in England and
Wales, whether directed towards clarification, reform or
abolition of the law of blasphemy. Many common law
jurisdictions retain an offence of blasphemy similar to
the common law of England and Wales, but there are others
which do not. Civil law systems either do not have a
comparable offence or have offences drafted in broad terms
in a fashion which might be regarded as unacceptable in
this country where it is the legislative tradition that
statutes creating criminal offences should state precisely
what it is that is prohibited. It is, however, worth
noting that in common law jurisdictions where codes have
recently been drafted or recommended, there has not been
any provision made for blasphemy.[197] Secondly, where
they already have such provisions, they have not been used
in recent times. In most instances, this must be a
consequence of executive policy with regard to institution
of proceedings, since, apart from England and Wales, control
of prosecutions is vested in the State. Finally, where,
as in India, the State has long had to cope with the
problems of a multi-religious society, it is significant
that, while there is no restriction upon what is meant by
"religion" in the relevant sections of the Code, the

---

197 See para. 4.5, above.

offences require proof of a stringent mental element.[198]

V   OTHER RELEVANT OFFENCES AND LEGAL CONTROLS

5.1   We now examine the scope of other offences which
have a close connection with blasphemy. Criminal libel
penalises anyone whose written publication of words tends to
injure the reputation of another, while seditious libel
penalises the written publication of words with a seditious
intention. Although these offences share a common ancestry
with blasphemous libel,[199] it would not now be appropriate
to use them in circumstances where the subject matter
complained of is the scurrilous treatment of the Christian
religion, and in the field of public order where seditious
libel was formerly widely used, there now exist modern
statutory offences. These two common law offences are in
any event already the subject of separate review.[200] Thus
by "other offences" we refer, not to other forms of libel
penalised by the criminal law nor to offences against
public worship, but to those penalising conduct which may
on occasion have a blasphemous element, principally the laws
relating to obscene publications and public order.

A.   Obscene Publications Act 1959

5.2   Section 2 of the Obscene Publications Act 1959
penalises anyone who, whether for gain or not, publishes
an obscene article, or has an obscene article for
publication for gain. "Publication", by virtue of section
1(3), includes distribution, sale, giving or lending, and

---

198   See paras. 4.10-4.11, above; compare Lord Scarman in
      Whitehouse v. Lemon [1979] A.C. 617, 658, and para.6.4,
      below.

199   See para. 2.3, above.

200   See para. 1.3, n.2, above.

in the case of films,[201] showing, playing or projecting;
and an article is by section 1(1) deemed to be obscene
if its effect is, if taken as a whole "such as to tend to
deprave and corrupt persons who are likely, having regard
to all relevant circumstances, to read, see or hear the
matter contained or embodied in it." An alternative
procedure under section 3 permits seizure under warrant of
articles suspected of being obscene and kept for publication
for gain, and the justices may order forfeiture unless
cause is shown why they should not be forfeited. Section 4
provides a defence of public good, under which a person is
not to be convicted, nor an order for forfeiture made, "if
it is proved that publication of the article in question is
justified as being for the public good on the ground that
it is in the interests of science, literature, art or
learning, or of other objects of general concern".[202]
Expert evidence is admissible to establish or negative any
such claim.[203] Similar provisions apply under the Theatres
Act 1968 to obscene performances of plays. The test of a
"tendency to deprave and corrupt" has been shown to be
unsatisfactory in practice and juries have tended not to
convict. This and other difficulties led to the review of

---

201 The Criminal Law Act 1977, s.53 has the effect of
extending the 1959 Act to films, with some
modifications. See generally (1976) Law Com. No. 76
Report on Conspiracy and Criminal Law Reform, Pt. III.

202 As to the interpretation of this provision, see Jordan
v. D.P.P. [1977] A.C. 699 and Attorney General's
Reference (No. 3 of 1977) [1978] 1 W.L.R. 1123.

203 Sect. 4(2).

204 Sects. 2 and 3. The consent of the Attorney General is
required for the institution of proceedings under this
Act: s.8. This was included, among other reasons,
because of the very serious consequences for
management and artists of any prosecution: see
Hansard (H.C.) 23 February 1968, Vol.759, col.867.

this area of the law in the <u>Report on Obscenity and Film Censorship</u>[205] (the "Williams Report"). There is an obvious parallel with the law of blasphemy here in so far as the jury are required to convict where there is proof beyond reasonable doubt of publication of matter defined in terms which are inherently uncertain in meaning. It may also be observed that, like the Obscene Publications Act, the law of blasphemy provides protection against the public availability of matter which many people may find offensive.[206]

5.3   Clearly, a blasphemous libel may in appropriate circumstances also constitute an obscene article within the meaning of the Obscene Publications Act 1959, even though obscenity is not an essential ingredient of blasphemous libel. So much is evident from <u>Whitehouse</u> v. <u>Lemon</u>: the defendants in that case were charged only with blasphemous libel,[207] but, as the Court of Appeal pointed out,[208] "[Counsel for the defendant] frankly admitted before us that had there been such a count [under the 1959 Act] the defendants might, subject of course to any defence under that statute, have been convicted of an offence against that Act". But leaving aside the possible element of a tendency to a breach of the peace, could all blasphemous libels be the subject of charges under the 1959 Act?

---

205 (1979) Cmnd. 7772. See para 5.4, below. Its terms of reference were "to review the laws concerning obscenity, indecency and violence in publications, displays and entertainments in England and Wales, except in the field of broadcasting, and to review the arrangements for film censorship in England and Wales; and to make recommendations".

206 See further para. 7.12, below.

207 Although the particulars referred to "a blasphemous libel ... namely an obscene poem ..."; see [1979] A.C. 617, 620.

208 [1979] Q.B. 10, 14.

On the constituent elements of the offence as we have
outlined them, it seems clear that a blasphemous libel does
not necessarily constitute an obscene article, as defined by
the 1959 Act. Although the Court of Appeal emphasised that
the jury in Lemon must have found the poem complained of
"obscene" in the ordinary meaning of that word,[209]
obscenity in the 1959 Act has the special and restricted
meaning of a tendency to deprave and corrupt. Furthermore,
the 1959 Act permits a defence of public good, while no such
defence is available in respect of blasphemous libel. Thus
in relation to the particular subject matter with which
blasphemous libel is concerned, that offence may be used to
penalise publications which would not be penalised under the
1959 Act.

5.4   The recommendations of the Williams Committee[210]
would, if implemented, effect fundamental changes in the
laws governing obscene publications. They would entail
repeal of the 1959 Act and of much of the legislation
outlined in paragraph 5.14, below in so far as it concerns
obscene and indecent publications. The written word would
be subject to no legal restrictions in regard to obscenity,
but restrictions would apply to any matter (other than
the printed word) and to any performance whose
unrestricted availability would be offensive to reasonable
people by reason of the manner in which it portrays,
deals with or relates to violence, cruelty or horror, or
sexual, faecal or urinary functions or genital organs.
These provisions would involve a ban on the display, sale,
hire etc. of restricted material and the presentation of

---

209   See Whitehouse v. Lemon [1979] Q.B. 10, 14; and as to
the "ordinary" usage of the term "obscene" in the
criminal law, see para. 5.14, below.

210   (1979) Cmnd. 7772. See in particular paras. 9.15,
9.18, 9.36, 9.41, 9.43, 9.50, 10.6 and 10.13.

any restricted performance save in premises excluding persons under eighteen, with warning notices and an absence of exterior display. Offences would penalise, inter alia, the display, sale or hire of restricted matter or presentation of a restricted performance in contravention of these conditions. Cases would be triable summarily with maximum penalties of six months' imprisonment and a fine of £1,000. The Report also recommends an absolute prohibition on certain photographs, films and live performances with offences triable on indictment for contravention of the prohibition, and the establishment of a statutory Film Examining Board to examine films intended for public exhibition. It is noteworthy that the Committee recommended that there should be no defence of public good[211] and that prosecution of the recommended summary offences should be undertaken only by the police or by or with the consent of the Director of Public Prosecutions, and of the recommended indictable offences only by or with the consent of the Director.[212]

5.5   In relation to the law of blasphemy, the Williams Committee said -[213]

> "the only recent instances in which the offence of blasphemy has been used (in the case of the publication by Gay News of a poem by James Kirkup) or the possibility of its being used has been in issue (principally as regards the projected film of the purported sex life of Christ) have been in a connection which falls plainly within the field we have been considering. We therefore express the view that the principles we have set out relating to harm and offensiveness apply equally to matter of this kind and that the

---

211 See Cmnd. 7772, paras. 9.41, 10.12 and 11.10.

212 Ibid., paras. 9.47-9.50, 10.20, 11.16 and 12.49. See also the Indecent Displays (Control) Bill, para. 7.19, below.

213 See Cmnd. 7772, para. 9.38.

appropriate way for the law to deal with such matter is through the scheme we have outlined here. We do not believe that the law should seek to restrain material of this kind if it does not offend against the test we have recommended and consequently we consider that in these connections there is no need for a separate offence of blasphemy. Whether there are other reasons for keeping an offence of blasphemy is not for us to decide."

The Committee therefore expressed no view in regard to blasphemous material which, while not offensive by the criterion adopted by the Committee,[214] might be considered offensive on other grounds.

B. Public Order Act 1936, section 5

5.6   In the field of public order, the principal offence requiring consideration is section 5 of the Public Order Act 1936.[215] As originally enacted, this penalised on summary conviction (with three months' imprisonment) anyone -

"who in any public place or at any public meeting uses threatening, abusive or insulting words or behaviour with intent to provoke a breach of the peace or whereby a breach of the peace is likely to be occasioned".

The offence became indictable under the Public Order Act 1963 with a maximum penalty of 12 months' imprisonment and a £500 fine. Section 7 of the Race Relations Act 1965 substituted a new section 5 in order to cover written material, and this was amended by the Criminal Law Act 1977 as a result of which it reverted to being a summary

---

214   See para. 5.4, above.

215   The Public Order Act 1936 is under review by the Home Office: see Review of the Public Order Act 1936 and related legislation (1980) Cmnd. 7891.

offence. Section 5 now provides that -

> "Any person who in any public place or at
> any public meeting
>
> (a) uses threatening, abusive or
>   insulting words or behaviour, or
>
> (b) distributes or displays any writing,
>   sign or visible representation which
>   is threatening, abusive or insulting,
>
> with intent to provoke a breach of the peace
> or whereby a breach of the peace is likely
> to be occasioned, shall be guilty of an
> offence and shall on summary conviction be
> liable to imprisonment for a term not
> exceeding six months or to a fine not
> exceeding £1000 or both."[216]

Clearly, there may be cases under section 5 which will
constitute blasphemous libel, and abusive and insulting
words which will constitute blasphemy. There are, however,
differences in the elements of these offences which
require careful consideration to establish the extent of
this overlap.

5.7   In the first place, so far as written material
is concerned section 5 penalises such material only where
it is distributed or displayed, whereas blasphemous libel
penalises publication. The latter undoubtedly covers,
for example, the sale in a bookshop of a publication
containing, but not displaying on its exterior, blasphemous
material. Whether section 5 does so is, however, doubtful.
Leaving aside the element of a breach of the peace,
although "distribution" may be wide enough to include
sale, and a bookshop certainly falls within the definition
of what constitutes a "public place" for the purposes of

---

216   The Metropolitan Police Act 1839, s. 54(13) and the
      City of London Police Act 1839, s. 35(13), applying
      respectively in the Metropolitan Police District and
      the City of London also provide summary offences with
      low, monetary penalities for using threatening,
      abusive or insulting words or behaviour.

section 5, paragraph (b) of that section was probably not
intended to deal with this situation. Moreover, as we
have seen,[217] distribution and sale are specified
separately under the Obscene Publications Act 1959. Thus
it may well be that sale by a bookshop of a blasphemous
publication not openly displaying matter which is
"abusive" or "insulting" is not penalised by section 5,
even if its contents are found on examination to have these
characteristics. A second distinction between the two
offences lies in the requirement of section 5 that the
prohibited acts must at least be likely to occasion a
breach of the peace. We have noted that in blasphemy this
requirement is either exiguous or non-existent.[218] There
are other differences which are of lesser significance.
Thus section 5 penalises conduct occurring only "in any
public place or at any public meeting"; there is no such
limitation in blasphemy. But the definition of "public
place" is extremely wide;[219] wide enough, as we have
pointed out, to encompass the display of material inside
a shop or the showing of a film in a cinema. Thus apart
from the question of broadcasts,[220] the limitation upon
section 5 is in this respect of no great importance in

---

217 See para. 5.2, above.

218 See paras. 3.3-3.4, above.

219 By s. 9(1) (as amended by the Criminal Justice Act
     1972, s. 33), "public place" includes any highway
     and any other premises or place to which at the
     material time the public have or are permitted to
     have access, whether on payment or otherwise;
     "public meeting" includes any meeting in a public
     place and any meeting which the public or any section
     thereof are permitted to attend, whether on payment
     or otherwise; and "meeting" means a meeting held for
     the purpose of the discussion of matters of public
     interest or for the purpose of the expression of
     views on such matters.

220 See para. 3.5, above, and para. 5.13, below.

the present context.[221] Again, under section 5 matter must be "threatening, abusive or insulting"; blasphemy requires that it must be "scurrilous", "vilifying", "abusive" or "insulting" in regard to Christ or the Christian religion. Here also the difference of substance is probably not great. "Insulting" in section 5 must be given its ordinary meaning which is not a question of law.[222] In both, what is insulting is a question of fact, but in blasphemy the publication must be found sufficiently insulting by the jury to be penalised.

5.8   We think that the most significant distinction between the two offences is that blasphemous libel is wide enough to penalise the _sale_ of certain books or other printed matter. There is no need for the _display_ of material which would then and there be likely to occasion

---

221   See also para. 3.1, above as to whether the place and circumstances should be taken into account in assessing whether blasphemous statements are punishable.

222   _Brutus_ v. _Cozens_ [1973] A.C. 854. Viscount Dilhorne (at pp. 865-866) stated that "it was relevant for [the magistrates] to consider whether the behaviour was such as to indicate an intention to insult anyone, and if so whom, and ... they may well have concluded that the appellant's behaviour did not evince any intention to insult either players or spectators, and so could not properly be regarded as insulting." It is possible to take the view that this indicates, first, that "insulting" here necessarily requires that the words be intended to insult a particular person or body of persons, and, secondly, that there must be an intent to insult or recklessness as to whether the words will insult (see as to the second point Smith and Hogan, _Criminal Law_ (4th ed., 1978) p. 762). In our view neither of these contentions is supported by the context in which they appear in Viscount Dilhorne's speech, as his remarks here were directed to the two questions of fact which the magistrates had to decide, namely, whether the appellant's behaviour was, objectively considered, insulting, and whether it was likely to occasion a breach of the peace. Nor are the contentions supported by the other speeches; see in particular Lord Morris of Borth-y-Gest at p. 864.

a breach of the peace, even if examination of the contents of such material at some later time might then induce its readers to take some action leading to a breach of the peace. On the other hand, we have suggested that by its limitation to distribution and display, the operation of section 5 is in practice likely to be restricted to material which on its face is likely to have some more immediate impact on the public peace. If we are correct in drawing this distinction, it serves to emphasise how remote the connection now is between the offence of blasphemy and the law relating to public order.[223] Clearly, the distinction will require further examination when we come to consider the grounds for retention of criminal sanctions upon blasphemy.[224]

C. Public Order Act 1936, section 5A

5.9   By section 5A of the Public Order Act 1936, added to that Act by section 70 of the Race Relations Act 1976 -

> "(1)   A person commits an offence if -
>
> (a)   he publishes or distributes written matter which is threatening, abusive or insulting;   or
>
> (b)   he uses in any public place or at any public meeting words which are threatening, abusive or insulting,
>
> in a case where, having regard to all the circumstances, hatred is likely to

---

223   Compare Whitehouse v. Lemon [1979] A.C. 617: blasphemous libel is an offence "designed to safeguard the internal tranquillity of the kingdom... in the field where the law seeks to safeguard public order and tranquillity" (per Lord Scarman at pp. 658 and 662).

224   See paras. 7.22-7.23, below.

be stirred up against any racial group in Great Britain by the matter or words in question."225

Institution of proceedings in England and Wales requires the consent of the Attorney General; and the maximum penalty on summary conviction is six months' imprisonment and a fine of £1000, and on indictment two years' imprisonment and a fine. While it is doubtful whether there are instances of blasphemy which would also constitute this offence, the provision is significant as an example of legislation limiting freedom of expression on grounds of public policy without the need to prove any immediate likelihood of a breach of the peace. By comparison with section 5, it is noteworthy also that the actus reus covers publication, as well as distribution, of written matter. The history of the provision[226] is relevant in two respects to our consideration of reform of the law of blasphemy: first, the absence from it of any subjective mental element, and, secondly, the absence from it of any reference to the stirring up of hatred against a group defined by reference to religious belief, as distinct from race.

---

225 As to the meaning of "public place" and "public meeting" see n. 219, above. By s. 5A(6), "publish" and "distribute" mean publish or distribute to the public at large or to any section of the public not consisting exclusively of members of an association of which the person publishing or distributing is a member; "written matter" includes any writing, sign or visible representation; "racial group" means a group of persons defined by reference to colour, race, nationality or ethnic or national origins.

226 See generally Leopold, "Incitement to Hatred - The History of a Controversial Criminal Offence" [1977] Public Law 389-405 and D.G.T. Williams "Racial Incitement and Public Order" [1966] Crim. L.R. 320-327 and the same author's Keeping the Peace, (1967) esp. Ch. 7.

5.10   Until 1965, there was no offence which specifically penalised incitement to racial hatred, despite several attempts to strengthen the law against such conduct, including an attempt by a number of Members of Parliament to have such an offence inserted when the Public Order Bill was before Parliament in 1936. Section 6(1) of the Race Relations Act 1965 provided, under the heading of "Public Order", an offence in which the conduct penalised was similar to what is now section 5A of the Public Order Act 1936, but requiring in addition an "intent to stir up hatred against any section of the public in Great Britain distinguished by colour, race or ethnic or national origins". The provision was part of a wider strategy to deal with what was regarded as the major social problem of easing the integration of the immigrant community. But the need to prove intent made successful prosecutions under it difficult to achieve.[227] As a result of criticisms, in particular those made by Lord Scarman in his Report of the Inquiry into the disorders in Red Lion Square,[228] section 6 of the 1965 Act was repealed[229] and replaced by section 70 of the Race Relations Act 1976, inserting the new section 5A in the Public Order Act 1936. This, as we have seen,[230] requires no proof of intent to stir up racial hatred. The significance of this change in the present context was that it was brought about by the practical necessity of dealing effectively with what was regarded as an urgent social problem.

---

227   According to the Home Secretary during the Second Reading debate on the Race Relations Bill 1976 these difficulties were increased by the enactment of section 8 of the Criminal Justice Act 1967 which made it necessary to prove a subjective intent: Hansard (H.C.) Vol. 906, col. 1563.

228   (1975) Cmnd. 5919, para. 125.

229   Race Relations Act 1976, Sch. 5.

230   See para. 5.9, above.

5.11   We have seen that section 5A penalises cases
where hatred is likely to be stirred up against any racial
group, by which is meant "a group of persons defined by
reference to colour, race, nationality or ethnic or
national origins".[231] It therefore does not extend to
cases where hatred is stirred up against persons on account
of their religion. Suggestions for such an offence have
been made on a number of occasions in recent years both
inside and outside Parliament.[232] During the committee
stage of the Race Relations Bill 1965, attempts were made
by some Members to widen clause 3 (which eventually became
section 6 of the 1965 Act) so that it would cover such
conduct. Concern was in particular expressed as to whether
Jews would be within the phrase "colour, race, or ethnic
or national origins." The Government sought to allay the
fears of those who were as concerned about possible
incitement against Jews as against racial groups by stating
that the clause was "quite wide enough to include people
of the Jewish religion".[233] In any event, the Government
were opposed to its widening, the Home Secretary stating
that -

> "If we are legislating about stirring up
> hatred against people for something they
> cannot help, it is permissible to be
> rather more drastic in our interference in
> what may be or may not be said than if we
> were legislating about stirring up hatred
> on grounds which people can help. People
> can change their religion.... It is utterly
> different from something which they cannot
> help, such as the colour of their skin."[234]

---

231 Public Order Act 1936, s. 5A(6).

232 Attempts were made to penalise such conduct when the
     Public Order Bill was before Parliament in 1936; see
     D.G.T. Williams, Keeping the Peace (1967) p. 169.

233 House of Commons, Standing Committee B (Race Relations
     Act) 27 May 1965, col. 83, (Sir Frank Soskice).

234 Ibid., cols. 82-83.

Furthermore, he added, there was no evidence of attempts in Great Britain to stir up hatred against people by reason of their religion as opposed to their racial origins. It is also highly relevant in the present context to note that the Government took the view that section 5 of the Public Order Act 1936 (as substituted by the Race Relations Act 1965, section 7) was perfectly adequate to deal with "the use of language of an insulting character directed by way of attack" on political _and religious_ beliefs.[235]

5.12   The Race Relations Act 1965 did not extend to Northern Ireland, but in this context it is worth noting the terms of the corresponding legislation now in force there.[236] Section 1 of the Prevention of Incitement to Hatred Act (Northern Ireland) 1970 provides that a person shall be guilty of an offence -

> "if, with intent to stir up hatred against, or arouse fear of, any section of the public in Northern Ireland -
>
> (a) he publishes or distributes written or other matter which is threatening, abusive or insulting; or
>
> (b) he uses in any public place or at any public meeting words which are threatening, abusive or insulting;
>
> being matters or words likely to stir up hatred against, or arouse fear of, any section of the public in Northern Ireland on grounds of religious belief, custom, race or ethnic or national origins" (emphasis added).

Despite the separate emphasis laid on religious belief, only one case appears to have been brought under it, and the

---

235 _Ibid._, col. 85.

236 See generally Leopold, "Incitement to Hatred - The History of a Controversial Criminal Offence" [1977] Public Law 389 at pp. 399 et _seq._

66

defendants were acquitted.[237]

D. Broadcasting

5.13   We have noted[238] that it is probable that radio
and television transmissions may be the subject of
proceedings for blasphemy and blasphemous libel. Thus
although they do not create criminal offences, it is
convenient to deal with the statutory provisions relevant
in this context. The most important provision is in
section 4(1)(a) of the Independent Broadcasting Authority
Act 1973, under which the Authority has a duty to satisfy
itself that, so far as possible, programmes broadcast by
it comply with the requirement that -

> "nothing is included in the programmes
> which offends against good taste or
> decency or is likely to encourage or
> incite to crime or lead to disorder or
> to be offensive to public feeling".

The duty was imposed on independent television at its
inception in 1954 and was included also in the Television
Act of 1964. At that date the BBC undertook by a letter
from the Chairman of its Board of Governors to the
Postmaster General to be bound by the same standards. This
undertaking was reaffirmed when the BBC Charter was renewed
in 1969, and the contents of the letter are noted in a
memorandum under the Licence Agreement.[239] The undertaking
is not legally enforceable; but in any event a system of

---

237 Leopold, op. cit., p. 401. The prosecution was brought
     against three members of the Shankill Defence
     Association in respect of a song in the Orange
     Loyalist Songs 1971 published by it. It failed because
     of the prosecution's inability to prove the necessary
     intent on the part of the defendants to incite hatred.

238 See para. 3.5, above.

239 Robertson, Obscenity (1979) pp. 270-271 and 343.

self-censorship is operated by both networks by means of internal controls.[240] It is also worth noting that the IBA is under a duty to ensure that there shall be no advertisement inserted by or on behalf of any body the objects of which are wholly or mainly of a religious nature, and none which is directed towards any religious end.[241]

E. Other offences

5.14   Other offences relevant in this context may be mentioned more briefly.

> 1. Section 4 of the Vagrancy Act 1824 penalises "every person wilfully exposing to view, in any street, road, highway or public place, any obscene print, picture or other indecent exhibition". This is extended by the Vagrancy Act 1838 to such exposure in shop windows or other parts of buildings situated on the public highway.[242] A defendant convicted under section 4 is liable to a maximum sentence of three months' imprisonment or a fine of £100.[243]

---

240 Ibid., pp. 271 et seq.; and see Attorney General ex rel. McWhirter v. I.B.A. [1973] Q.B. 629.

241 Independent Broadcasting Authority Act, s. 8 and Sch. 2, para. 8.

242 The Indecent Displays (Control) Bill (n. 348, below) schedules for repeal both these provisions and those in the Metropolitan Police Act 1839 and the Town Police Clauses Act 1847 relating to indecent and obscene publications outlined in para. 5.14(2), below.

243 Magistrates' Courts Act 1952, s. 27(3) and Criminal Justice Act 1967, s. 93 (raised to £200 under the Magistrates' Courts Act 1980, s. 34(3)). Sect. 5 of the Vagrancy Act 1824 permits higher penalties to be imposed by the Crown Court if the offences are repeated.

2. Section 54(12) of the Metropolitan Police
Act 1839, and section 35(12) of the City
of London Police Act 1839 penalise anyone
selling or exhibiting to public view any
"profane, indecent, or obscene" publication
and anyone who "to the annoyance of the
inhabitants or passengers" sings any "profane,
indecent or obscene song or ballad", or
writes or draws "any indecent or obscene
word, figure or representation" or uses
"any profane, indecent or obscene" language.
Section 28 of the Town Police Clauses Act
1847, which applies elsewhere wherever it
has been adopted, is similarly comprehensive,
albeit drafted in simpler terms. The
maximum penalty under the Metropolitan Police
Act is a fine of £50, under the two other
Acts £20.[244] We deal with these provisions
in greater detail in Part XI of this Paper.

3. Insulting conduct at places of religious
worship and burial is penalised under
section 2 of the Ecclesiastical Courts
Jurisdiction Act 1860. This is examined in
Part XII of this Paper.

4. Section 42 of the Customs Consolidation Act
1876 prohibits importation of "indecent or
obscene prints, paintings, photographs,
books, cards, lithographic or other
engravings, or any other indecent or obscene
articles".[245]

---

244 See Criminal Justice Act 1967, Sch. 3, Criminal Law
Act 1977, Sch. 6.

245 Such importation may lead to forfeiture or criminal
proceedings: see Customs and Excise Management Act
1979, ss. 49-50 and s. 170.

5. Section 3 of the Indecent Advertisements Act 1889 penalises anyone who affixes in a public place or exhibits to public view in the window of any house or shop "any picture or written matter which is of an indecent or obscene nature...." The maximum penalty is a fine of £20.[246]

6. Section 11 of the Post Office Act 1953 creates an offence of sending, attempting to send or procuring to be sent a postal packet (i) enclosing any indecent or obscene print etc. or article, or (ii) which has on it or on its cover any words etc. grossly offensive or of an indecent or obscene character. The maximum penalty on summary conviction is £100,[247] and on indictment 12 months' imprisonment. Section 78 of the Post Office Act 1969 penalises sending by means of a public telecommunication service a message or other matter that is "grossly offensive or of an indecent, obscene or menacing character". The maximum penalty on summary conviction is a fine of £50.

7. Section 4 of the Unsolicited Goods and Services Act 1971 penalises the unsolicited sending to another of books etc. or advertising material describing or illustrating human sexual techniques. The maximum penalty on summary conviction is a fine of £100 for the first offence and £400 for any subsequent offence, and

---

246 To be repealed by the Indecent Displays (Control) Bill.

247 Ibid. Sect. 68 makes it an offence to solicit or endeavour to procure any other person to commit such an offence.

institution of proceedings requires the
consent of the Director of Public Prosecutions.

8. A wide range of conduct is penalised by
    common law offences, including conspiracies
    to corrupt public morals and outrage public
    decency, public exhibition of indecent acts
    and things, keeping a disorderly house,
    obscene libel and conspiracy to debauch.
    These were examined in detail in Part III
    of our Report on Conspiracy and Criminal
    Law Reform[248] in which we recommended their
    abolition. This part of the Report was not
    implemented by the Criminal Law Act 1977
    because of the need for a more wide-ranging
    review of the laws relating to obscenity
    than our terms of reference permitted; that
    review was undertaken by the Williams
    Committee.

Apart from those outlined in subparagraphs 3 and 7, these
offences penalise "obscene" matter in various ways. In
the context of section 11 of the Post Office Act 1953,
"obscene" bears its ordinary dictionary meaning, that is,
"shocking, lewd, indecent and so on,"[249] as distinct from
its special meaning under the Obscene Publications Act
1959.[250] Some, but not all, blasphemous conduct will

---

248 (1976) Law Com. No. 76. Sect. 5(3) of the Criminal
    Law Act 1977 preserves the conspiracy offences at
    common law, although, as we explained in Law Com.
    No. 76 (paras. 3.21-3.23), it is possible that there
    are also generic common law offences of corrupting
    public morals and outraging public decency irrespective
    of the element of conspiracy.

249 R. v. Anderson [1972] 1 Q.B. 304, 311-312 per
    Widgery L.C.J. (the "Oz" case).

250 See para. 5.3, above.

therefore be covered by one or other of these offences,[251] although the maximum penalties under the statutes we have referred to are lower than that for blasphemous libel. It should also be noted that, were the recommendations of the Williams Committee Report on Obscenity and Film Censorship[252] to be implemented, the common law offences specified in subparagraph 8 would, in so far as they deal with printed material and indecent performances, be superseded.

5.15   The preceding paragraphs indicate that there is some overlap between the conduct penalised by the offences there outlined and the conduct penalised by the law of blasphemy. Nevertheless, we have indicated[253] that not all cases of blasphemy and blasphemous libel are covered by other offences. Whether the abolition of blasphemy and blasphemous libel would in consequence leave a gap in the law which needs to be filled is the question which we consider after discussing what in our view are the principal defects of the present law.

VI   DEFECTS OF THE PRESENT LAW

A.   Uncertainty

6.1   Our description of the present law[254] has indicated that the offence of blasphemous libel is potentially wide in scope but uncertain in application. Once the judge has directed the jury as to the ingredients of the offence, it

---

251   See para. 5.4, above, where we noted the comment of the Court of Appeal in Whitehouse v. Lemon that the jury must have found the poem complained of "obscene" in the ordinary meaning of that word. In 1977, after the decision of the trial judge in Lemon a successful prosecution was brought under section 11 of the Post Office Act 1953 against a secularist who sent a copy of the Gay News poem through the post: Robertson, Obscenity (1979), p. 242.

252   (1979) Cmnd. 7772; see para. 5.4, above.

253   See in particular para. 5.8, above.

254   Part III, above.

is for the jury to say whether the matter is "scurrilous"
or "abusive" or "insulting" in relation to the Christian
religion and thereby has a tendency to induce a breach of
the peace. On the criterion advanced by the trial judge in
Lemon[255] the requirement of a "tendency to a breach of the
peace" is so vestigial as to be of little consequence; and
in Lord Scarman's view,[256] the requirement disappears
altogether. Thus it is hardly an exaggeration to say that
whether or not a publication is a blasphemous libel can only
be judged ex post facto. It is blasphemous if at least 10
out of 12 members of the jury[257] think it is sufficiently
"scurrilous", "abusive" or "offensive" in regard to the
Christian religion. Delimitation of a criminal offence by
reference to jury application of one or more of several
adjectives (all of which recessitate subjective interpretation
and none of which is absolute) is hardly satisfactory. In
the result we think it is likely to be difficult if not
impossible to prophesy in any particular case what the
verdict may be. This has serious consequences. It is
desirable that all areas of the criminal law should pay some
respect to the objective of certainty, in the sense that it
should be possible to determine in advance with at least a
reasonable degree of likelihood whether particular conduct
will constitute an offence or not.[258] There is no such
likelihood in the case of the present law of blasphemy.
This shortcoming is not merely of academic interest· In
its written form the offence is a libel, and it is therefore
important from the point of view of commercial enterprises -
whether these be the publishers of books or periodicals or
the makers of films or television programmes[259] - to ensure

---

255 See para. 3.3, above.

256 Ibid.

257 Lemon was decided on a majority verdict: see
     para. 2.15, above.

258 As to this aspect, see the judgment of the European
     Court of Human Rights in the Sunday Times case,
     quoted in para. 6.6, below.

259 See para. 7.25, below.

that, as in the case of other forms of libel, the bounds set
by the law are not exceeded. Yet since the law is so uncertain
in ambit, it becomes, to say the least, difficult for any
legal advice to be given as to whether or not a jury in
whichever part of the country a prosecutor (who may be a
private prosecutor) institutes proceedings will find a
particular publication blasphemous. While matter which is
merely abusive is ignored in the law of defamatory libel, it
becomes of the essence in blasphemous libel, provided that the
jury finds it sufficiently scurrilous to amount to the offence.

6.2   This uncertainty is virtually unaffected even if,
contrary to the views of Lord Scarman,[260] a tendency to a
breach of the peace is accepted as a necessary element of the
offence. As we have seen, if this element survives, it means
in this context no more than that the publication must be such
as "to provoke or arouse angry feelings, something which is a
possibility, not a probability".[261] If blasphemy is to be
regarded as an offence "designed to safeguard the internal
tranquillity of the kingdom", which according to the most
recent authority is still its primary function,[262] the
exiguous or non-existent burden laid upon the prosecution to
prove some possibility of disturbance to public order compares
unfavourably with the position in other areas of the law. We
mention here only two instances: first, the duty laid upon a
constable to prevent a breach of the peace which he reasonably
apprehends, to which we have already referred;[263] and
secondly, the limits imposed by section 5 of the Public Order
Act 1936, where a subjective intent to cause a breach of the
peace or an objective likelihood of a breach of the peace is

---

260 See para. 3.3, above.

261 R. v. Lemon, per Judge King-Hamilton Q.C., transcript of
     summing-up, p. 11a; and see paras. 2.15 and 3.3, above.

262 See Whitehouse v. Lemon [1979] A.C. 617, at pp. 658 and
     662 per Lord Scarman.

263 See para. 3.4, above.

required.[264] If the requirements of section 5 were held to be satisfied by a requirement that the behaviour complained of might possibly, not probably, arouse angry feelings, we believe that its unacceptable character would be readily apparent and that it would be regarded as a gross infringement of freedom of expression.

B. Strict liability

6.3   As we have noted,[265] in consequence of the decision of the House of Lords in <u>Whitehouse</u> v. <u>Lemon</u>[266] the only intention which need be proved for the offence is an intention to publish; the defendant need not intend any consequence or effects, and no other intention as to the effect of the words in question is relevant. The dissenting minority in the House of Lords thought that, by so excluding the necessity to prove an intent to blaspheme on the part of the publisher, the effect of the majority's decision was to make the offence one of strict liability.[267] The majority, however, thought that this was not so.[268] Professor Smith has criticised[269] the majority's reasoning on this point:

> "There is no universally accepted criterion of what amounts to strict liability. Virtually all offences require some mental element. The

---

264 See para. 5.6, above. As to authority on what constitutes a likelihood of a breach of the peace, see <u>Bryan</u> v. <u>Robinson</u> [1960] 1 W.L.R. 506 (on s.54(13) of the Metropolitan Police Act 1839, para. 5.6, above) and <u>Maile</u> v. <u>McDowell</u> [1980] Crim. L.R. 580; and for the view that <u>this</u> term is "hardly a limiting factor in the use of s. 5", see Bevan, "Protest and Public Order" [1979] Public Law p. 163 at pp. 180-183. See also <u>Simcock</u> v. <u>Rhodes</u> (1977) 66 Cr. App. R. 192.

265 See para. 3.8, above.

266 [1979] A.C. 617.

267 [1979] A.C. 617, 637-638 (Lord Diplock), 656 (Lord Edmund-Davies).

268 <u>Ibid</u>., 639-640 (Viscount Dilhorne), 657 (Lord Russell), 662 (Lord Scarman).

269 [1979] Crim. L.R. at p. 312; see also J.R. Spencer, [1979] C.L.J. p. 249.

offence committed in the leading case on strict liability, Prince[270] requires proof of a very substantial element. It is thus misleading to say that strict liability offences 'require no mens rea'. The truth is that they require proof of a limited degree of mens rea.... If a man who is unaware of it is liable to be convicted of blasphemy, then he is held strictly liable in precisely the same way as the butcher who sells meat which, though he neither knows, nor has reason to know it, is unfit for human consumption."

Having regard to the accepted definition of the actus reus, we agree with the minority and with Professor Smith that as a result of the decision the offence of blasphemy can now properly and fairly be regarded as one of strict liability. Furthermore, whether or not it is considered to be so, the absence of mens rea as to such an important part of the actus reus of the offence runs contrary to the general principle developed during the past century that mens rea is normally required as to all the elements of the actus reus both in common law and statutory crimes, save in special cases of regulatory offences.[271]

6.4   The development of this general principle has in our view in no way been weakened by the "movement of the law" in a contrary sense for which Lord Scarman argued in Whitehouse v. Lemon.[272] Lord Scarman stated that this movement embodies a tendency to make criminally liable "people who know what they are doing" in the absence of any intent by

---

270   (1875) L.R. 2 C.C.R. 114.

271   "The climate of both parliamentary and judicial opinion has been growing less favourable to the recognition of absolute offences over the last few decades; a trend to which section 1 of the Homicide Act 1957 and section 8 of the Criminal Justice Act 1967 bear witness in the case of Parliament, and in the case of the judiciary, is illustrated by the speeches in this House in Sweet v. Parsley [1970] A.C. 132" (R. v. Sheppard [1980] 3 W.L.R. 960 per Lord Diplock at p. 968].

272   See para. 2.19, above. Lord Scarman's speech, and in particular this part of it, is strongly criticised by J.R. Spencer in [1979] C.L.J. at pp. 248-249.

them to do the things which the laws cited by him[273] prohibit.
It is possible to take the view that the ambiguity of the
quoted phrase disguises the point at issue. For example,
does it mean "knowing that he is publishing the matter in
question" or "knowing that he is publishing the matter in
question, and knowing it to be blasphemous"? In any event, we
suggest that more significant movements of the law in recent
times are represented by section 8 of the Criminal Law Act
1967,[274] which substitutes "the subjective for the objective
test in applying the presumption that a man intends the
natural consequences of his acts",[275] and by decisions which
indicate a "move away from strict liability in relation both
to statutory offences and to common law crimes".[276] Nor
does the conclusion which Lord Scarman draws from his thesis,
to the effect that blasphemous libel requires no intent to
blaspheme, appear to be entirely compatible with comments
elsewhere in his speech; for in drawing attention to the
needs of a "plural society", he mentioned the position in
India where, as we have noted, the offences in question
require proof of a stringent mental element.[277]

6.5   In support of his contention, Lord Scarman referred
to the Obscene Publications Act 1959; but we have observed
that criticisms of the way in which that Act has worked led
to comprehensive new proposals for legislation by the
Williams Committee.[278] He also cited section 5A of the
Public Order Act 1936; but this was inserted by the Race
Relations Act 1976 because of the practical necessity for

---

273 See paras. 2.19, above and 6.5, below.

274 See n. 103, above.

275 See Whitehouse v. Lemon [1979] A.C. 617, 637 (per Lord
     Diplock).

276 Ibid., at p. 656 (per Lord Edmund-Davies).

277 See paras. 4.10-4.11, above, and para. 8.11, below.

278 See paras. 5.2-5.4, above.

dealing effectively with an urgent social problem.[279]
Whether it can be maintained that there is a
correspondingly urgent problem in the field of religious
belief is a matter which we consider below.[280]

6.6   Lord Scarman also referred to Articles 9 and
10 of the European Convention on Human Rights. Article 9
(the right to freedom of religion) implied, in his view,
a duty to refrain from insulting the religious feelings
of others; but, taking the article as a whole,[281] it may
be doubted whether such an implication can properly be
drawn, and indeed whether freedom to practise a religion
can imply an obligation to make it an offence to stop
others commenting on it in any way they choose.[282] Again,
while Article 10 (the right to freedom of expression)
does, as Lord Scarman says, carry under it "duties and
responsibilities" and is subject to certain limitations,

---

279   See para. 5.10, above.

280   See para. 7.15, below.

281   Article 9(1): "Everyone has the right to freedom of
      thought, conscience and religion; this right
      includes freedom to change his religion or belief and
      freedom, either alone or in community with
      others and in public or private, to manifest his
      religion or belief, in worship, teaching, practice
      and observance".

      Article 9(2): "Freedom to manifest one's religion
      or beliefs shall be subject only to such limitations
      as are presented by law and are necessary in a
      democratic society in the interests of public safety,
      for the protection of public order, health or morals,
      or for the protection of the rights and freedoms of
      others".

282   See "Intention to Blaspheme" (1979) 129 New L.J.
      pp. 205-206 and commentary on Whitehouse v. Lemon by
      Professor J.C. Smith in [1979] Crim. L.R. at pp. 313-
      314.

it may be doubted whether, read as a whole,[283] these
limitations have any bearing on the issue. If indeed
they are relevant in the present context, it seems to us
that they would limit freedom to comment on political and
any other beliefs just as much as on religious beliefs.
Furthermore, according to the decision of the European
Court of Human Rights in the Sunday Times case,[284] in the
context of deciding whether restrictions were "necessary
in a democratic society" in the circumstances of that
case, there was no question of balancing the interest in
freedom of expression against competing interests: there
was one principle, freedom of expression, which was
subject to a number of exceptions which must be narrowly
interpreted. And in deciding whether a particular
restriction upon freedom of expression was "prescribed by
law", "the citizen must be able to have an indication
that is adequate in the circumstances of the legal rules
applicable to a given case" and they must be "formulated
with sufficient precision to enable the citizen

---

283 By Art. 10(2) "The exercise of these freedoms, since
     it carries with it duties and responsibilities, may
     be subject to such formalities, conditions,
     restrictions or penalties as are prescribed by law
     and are necessary in a democratic society, in the
     interests of national security, territorial integrity
     or public safety, for the prevention of disorder or
     crime, for the protection of health or morals, for
     the protection of the reputation or rights of others,
     for preventing the disclosure of information received
     in confidence, or for maintaining the authority and
     impartiality of the judiciary".

284 The Sunday Times v. United Kingdom (1979) 2 E.H.R.R.
     245, 281. And see (1979) 129 New L.J. p. 508, I.C.J.
     Review, Dec. 1979 p. 64 and (1979) 123 Sol. J.
     pp. 416-417; see also Lord Diplock in Gleaves v.
     Deakin [1980] A.C. 477 at pp. 482-484. Compare
     Attorney General v. B.B.C. [1980] 3 W.L.R. 109, 127
     per Lord Fraser of Tullybelton. The defendant in
     Whitehouse v. Lemon has appealed to the European
     Commission on Human Rights alleging, among other
     grounds, that his conviction contravened Articles
     9(1) and 10(2): see The Guardian, 17 January 1981.

to regulate his conduct; he must be able - if need be
with appropriate advice - to foresee, to a degree that
is reasonable in the circumstances, the consequences
which a given action may entail". We express no view as
to whether, having regard to the uncertain bounds of the
law of blasphemy, this decision indicates that that
offence is incompatible with Article 10; but we suggest
that it detracts from the force of Lord Scarman's
citation of that Article in support of his contention. In
short, we are unable to agree that the "movement of the
law" which Lord Scarman detected can readily be
demonstrated either by the instances he cites or at all.

6.7   The practical consequence of the exclusion of
any requirement as to the intent of the defendant to
blaspheme is that he cannot give admissible evidence as
to what he claims to be his beliefs and purpose.[285] It
is thus quite possible for the offence to be committed by
someone with profound religious beliefs and with entirely
sincere motives, provided that the language in which he
expresses himself is sufficiently shocking and insulting
to be held blasphemous by a jury. Explanations
purporting to justify this were advanced by the majority
in Whitehouse v. Lemon.[286] For example, Viscount Dilhorne
suggested that to require proof of intention would be
going some way to making a defendant judge in his own
cause.[287] We doubt whether this argument can be sustained.
A requirement of a mental element of intent to blaspheme
in the offence of blasphemous libel would no more make a

---

285 See Whitehouse v. Lemon [1979] Q.B. 10, 16 and 27-28
     (C.A.) and [1979] A.C. 617, 657 (Lord Russell) and
     665 (Lord Scarman).
286 [1979] A.C. 617, 645 (Viscount Dilhorne), 657 (Lord
     Russell) and 665 (Lord Scarman).
287 Ibid., at p. 645.

defendant judge in his own cause than would the requirement of a mental element in other crimes or, for instance, the requirement that a defendant charged with theft must have an intention of permanently depriving the owner of the property in question. In all such cases evidence by the defendant of his state of mind is admissible and, as Viscount Dilhorne himself elsewhere recognised,[288] it would be for the jury, properly directed, to indicate by their verdict whether or not they believed the defendant in the light of the evidence as a whole.[289] Viscount Dilhorne's observation seems to us to amount to an argument against the requirement of a mental element in any crime, rather than against its absence from blasphemous libel alone.

6.8   It is in this context particularly easy to confuse the concepts of intention to blaspheme and the objective of the defendant, for example to increase circulation, which raises an issue of motive. The temptation to do so appears not to have been entirely avoided in Whitehouse v. Lemon.[290] But it is one of the tasks of counsel and trial judge to clarify them at the trial of any case where the defendant is accused of an offence requiring subjective intent. Yet given that none of these issues would raise especial difficulties in cases of blasphemy, it might still be queried, as the Court of Appeal did in Lemon,[291] whose intent would be relevant, that of the author (perhaps deceased), or anyone concerned with publication, or of the editor of the

---

288   Ibid., at p. 645.
289   See Criminal Law Act 1967, s. 8; and see on this point Orchard, "Blasphemy and Mens Rea" [1979] N.Z. Law J. p. 347 at p. 349.
290   See [1979] A.C. 617, at pp. 645 (Viscount Dilhorne) and 665 (Lord Scarman).
291   [1979] Q.B. 10, 27-28.

publication? Lord Edmund-Davies in his dissenting speech in <u>Whitehouse</u> v. <u>Lemon</u> was quite clear in his reply to this last point and distinguished clearly between intent and motive:[292] the intent to blaspheme -

> "must be brought home in turn to each person
> charged. If he is the author, the all-
> important question is what was his state of
> mind in supplying the material for publication;
> if he is the editor or publisher of the words
> of another, it is as to their state of mind
> in playing their respective roles in the act
> of publishing. And it would be nihil ad rem
> that one or all of them were motivated by,
> for example, the desire to make money or to
> make known the blasphemous words of another".

C.   Restriction to Christianity

6.9   Another shortcoming - or at any rate an anomaly
- in the present law of blasphemy is the narrow scope of
its protection. As we have seen,[293] it is clear that that
protection does not extend beyond the Christian religion,
but it is less clear whether in the law of England and
Wales it also protects the tenets of Christian
denominations other than the established Church. Having
regard to the authorities, it seems probable that at most
other denominations are protected only to the extent that
their fundamental beliefs are those which are held in
common with the established Church. It is less likely
that the present law affords any protection in respect of
beliefs not so held, for example, the special place held
by the Virgin Mary in the beliefs of certain denominations
of the Christian religion. An offence restricted in this
particular way is difficult to justify in modern
conditions. Whether its anomalous character argues for
its abolition or its extension is one of the principal
matters which we have to consider. Lord Scarman in

---

292 See [1979] A.C. 617, 656.
293 See para. 3.2, above.

<u>Whitehouse</u> v. <u>Lemon</u> took the latter view:

> "there is a case for legislation extending
> it [blasphemous libel] to protect the
> religious beliefs and feelings of non-
> Christians.... My criticism of the common
> law offence of blasphemy is not that it
> exists but that it is not sufficiently
> comprehensive. It is shackled by the chains
> of history".[294]

D. Can the defects be cured by a requirement of consent to prosecution?

6.10   In our view, the shortcomings described in the
foregoing paragraphs amply justify the view that the law
of blasphemy should not be left in its present state. It
may, however, be asked whether any defects might be cured
by making the institution of proceedings dependent upon
the prior consent of the Attorney General or Director
of Public Prosecutions. This possibility is of particular
relevance having regard to the suggestion by the House of
Lords that provision of such consent ought to be considered
in relation to the offence of criminal libel.[295] The
major defect which this would help to cure would be
inconsistencies in the decision whether or not to prosecute.
But we do not believe that this kind of restriction is a
satisfactory means of curing defects in the substance of
the law. The normal procedures at present used for

---

294   [1979] A.C. 617, 658.

295   See Gleaves v. <u>Deakin</u> [1980] A.C. 477 at pp. 484
      (Lord Diplock), 488 (Viscount Dilhorne), 493 (Lord
      Edmund-Davies), 496 (Lord Scarman). As we have noted,
      (para. 3.7, above), both blasphemous and criminal
      libel at present require leave of a High Court judge
      for institution of proceedings for libels published in
      newspapers, but, as Viscount Dilhorne said in <u>Gleaves</u>
      v. <u>Deakin</u> (<u>ibid</u>, at p. 488), "I do not myself <u>regard</u>
      it as very desirable that judges should have any
      responsibility for the institution of prosecutions."
      And see n. 150, above.

institution of proceedings may make the provision of consent desirable in cases where exceptional considerations of public policy necessarily play a part in the decision whether or not proceedings should be instituted, where it is desirable to ensure that there is a greater than usual degree of uniformity in the criteria applied in the decision to institute proceedings or, indeed, where there is a danger of frequent prosecution of trivial cases. But consent provisions are not in our view a satisfactory means of curing substantive defects in the law itself. Where, as in blasphemy, there is uncertainty as to the ambit of the offence, provision of a requirement of executive consent would in practical terms go a long way towards deciding at what point the law should impose criminal sanctions;[296] and in this particular offence, this in substance would mean deciding what limits are to be set to freedom of expression. This is in our view quite unacceptable; as Lord Reid remarked in a similar context, "A bad law is not defensible on the ground that it will be judiciously adminstered".[297]

6.11   We indicated at the outset of this paper,[298] that, since our objective of codifying the criminal law necessarily entails the abolition of offences at common law, blasphemy could not be retained in its present form.

---

296 A jury might of course disagree with the view taken by the Attorney General or D.P.P., but where the question of publication is seldom in issue and the sole criterion of guilt is so uncertain, it is more likely than not that there would be a conviction.

297 Knuller v. D.P.P. [1973] A.C., 435, 458-459; Lord Reid was here discussing the disadvantages of the offence of outrage to public decency, the existence of which was denied by him and Lord Diplock but upheld by Lord Simon of Glaisdale and Lord Kilbrandon.

298 See para. 1.2, above.

In considering what kind of offence, if any, should
replace the common law, the shortcomings of the existing
law described in the foregoing paragraphs will have to be
borne in mind. Whether there is a need for such a
replacement is, however, the most important issue for
consideration, and it is to this topic that we now turn.

VII   CONSIDERATION OF THE NEED FOR CRIMINAL SANCTIONS

A.   Preliminary considerations

7.1   Several preliminary matters need explanation
or emphasis. In the first place, it is clear that if
there were a complete overlap between the conduct penalised
by other offences and the conduct penalised by blasphemy,
the case for retaining criminal sanctions specifically
penalising blasphemy would be very considerably weakened.
But we have shown that, although there is a considerable
overlap of this kind, it is not complete, and that,
particularly in the sphere of public order, it will be
necessary to consider whether the restrictive character
of the relevant offences justifies special provisions
dealing with blasphemous material.[299] On the other hand,
in so far as blasphemous publications may be obscene or
indecent, there is a wide range of offences which are
appropriate to deal with them.[300] In asserting that they
are "appropriate" we are not commenting upon the adequacy
of those offences: the admitted need for their reform has
led to their recent examination, and we have noted that
the Williams Committee has recommended that the principles
advocated by it should be applied to blasphemous material

---

299   See paras. 5.8, above and 7.22-7.23, below.
300   See paras. 5.2-5.3 and 5.14, above.

which is harmful or offensive on the criteria it adopts.[301]
The relevant point here is that, given the existence of
offences relating to obscenity etc., the justification
for criminal sanctions must be sought elsewhere.

7.2   As a background to consideration of the arguments,
it is also relevant to note the response to our preliminary
consultation upon the subject, which we undertook shortly
after the House of Lords' decision in Whitehouse v. Lemon.[302]
It is our normal practice to seek the views of the public
through the medium of Working Papers, but several reasons
prompted us in this instance to make a preliminary request
for views. First, we thought that it would be useful to
inform the public that we were giving our attention to
blasphemy. Secondly, we recognised that the subject was
particularly sensitive, so that an opportunity for the
public to express its immediate response to the decision
seemed appropriate. Finally, Lord Scarman had made some
widely-reported observations upon the law,[303] in particular
suggesting that the law of blasphemy should apply to
religions other than Christianity, and we felt that public
response to this suggestion would be of particular interest.
Accordingly we sent letters to the press inviting the public
to send us their views with regard to the place of
blasphemy in the law today, the need for such an offence,
and its requirements.[304] We received some 170 letters and
submissions in reply from organisations and individuals.
A majority who wrote individual letters commented adversely

---

301 See para. 5.5, above; and see further para. 7.19,
     below.

302 [1979] A.C. 617.

303 [1979] A.C. 617, 658; see para. 6.9, above.

304 Letters in substantially the same terms were published
     in 1979 in the Daily Telegraph, the Financial Times,
     the Guardian, the Observer, New Society, Guardian
     Gazette, New Law Journal and Solicitors Journal.

and in detail upon the law, considering it to be archaic
in modern conditions and an unnecessary check upon freedom
of expression;[305] and a small number of practising
Christians stated that they were so outraged by the recent
prosecution in Whitehouse v. Lemon and the absence of
condemnation by the Church of what they regarded as an
example of unacceptable intolerance, that they had ceased
to be communicant members of the Church of England. A
substantial minority, however, favoured the retention of a
law of blasphemy and a few favoured the extension of the
law to religions other than Christianity. Of those
favouring retention, many wanted a law not only more
extensive in scope but one which would in practice be more
frequently invoked than the common law offence. It is
clear that most of those who commented in this spirit did
not appreciate the present bounds of the common law which,
uncertain though it is, only penalises matter which is
"scurrilous" or "vilifying". Their complaints were in many
instances of "blasphemy" in everyday life and in the media,
particularly on television and radio; and from this it is
evident that the term was understood in its wider,
dictionary sense of "impious or profane talk".[306] Any
criminal sanctions capable of penalising such language
would plainly be far wider than the present common law of
blasphemy and a different type of offence altogether.

---

305 Although the view has been expressed that much of the
concern caused by Whitehouse v. Lemon stemmed from
special pleading by small groups with a particular
interest, we received only a few letters from the "Gay
rights" movement. On the other hand, a substantial
number of those who wrote to advocate retention of the
law of blasphemy appeared to have done so in response
to suggestions by the National Viewers' and Listeners'
Association.

306 Concise Oxford Dictionary (6th ed., 1976); this
definition was actually quoted by one correspondent.

7.3   Finally, in considering justifications for legal sanctions, we do not at this stage postulate that these sanctions should take any particular form: the issue is whether criminal sanctions of any kind are justifiable. If we conclude that the sanctions of the criminal law are needed, their content is a matter which requires separate consideration in the light of the arguments which appear to be most cogent.

7.4   It is necessary at the outset to state that the viewpoints of those favouring criminal sanctions and those opposing them seem to us fundamentally incapable of reconciliation. Arguments in favour of criminal sanctions give primacy in the scale of values to religion and religious beliefs as matters of supreme importance to society as a whole; they must from this point of view be defended from what are regarded as attacks upon them. To those for whom blasphemous conduct is profoundly unacceptable and morally "wrong", no debate about the proper function of the criminal law which is confined solely to utilitarian arguments is likely to prove convincing. On the other hand, those not sharing this outlook will point to the need to maintain freedom of speech unless there are overwhelming reasons of social necessity which require a curb to be imposed in a particular area. Such curbs exist in the sphere of public order, which it is the primary function of the criminal law to maintain; they exist also in the sphere of civil defamation subject to defences of justification, privilege and fair comment. Opponents of criminal sanctions may ask what reasons of commensurate importance can support curbs upon liberty of speech if these considerations are not present. We take as our starting point the arguments put forward in debate, both in the press and in Parliament,[307] and by some of our correspondents. The arguments supporting criminal sanctions

---

307 See the debate on the Blasphemy Bill, Hansard (H.L.) (1978) Vol. 389, cols. 279-350; see para. 2.25 above.

seem to fall under four broad headings which we examine
in turn.

B. Arguments for the maintenance of criminal sanctions

1. The protection of religion and religious beliefs

7.5   At its most general level, the law is regarded
as protecting the Deity and Christian institutions and
beliefs from affront and attack, irrespective of whether
offence is caused to the feelings of believers. This viewpoint was expressed in a number of letters from our
correspondents: blasphemous conduct was an "affront" to or
a "grave offence" against God and "disobedience to His
command"; it was far graver to refer in derogatory terms
to the Son of God than to members of the community
distinguished by their colour or nationality. The
viewpoint was one which was implicit in all the cases up to
Bradlaugh and Ramsay and Foote.[308] Today, it is perhaps

---

308   (1883) 15 Cox C.C. 217 and 231; see para. 2.8, above.
As we noted there, Lord Coleridge's definition of the
actus reus in blasphemy did not differ from that in
R. v. Hetherington (1841) 4 St. Tr. N.S. 563; see
para. 2.5, above. The difference lay in Lord
Coleridge's further dictum that the jury had to decide
whether the indicted libels "are not calculated and
intended to insult the feelings and the deepest
religious convictions of the great majority of persons
amongst whom we live"; (1883) 15 Cox C.C. at p. 230.
"What was novel in Coleridge's judgment was not his
willingness to take account of the character of an
attack upon Christianity, but his willingness to do so
in such a way that the object of the legal protection
became Christian believers rather than Christian
belief": Jones, "Blasphemy, Offensiveness and Law",
(1980) B.J. Pol. S. 10, p. 129 at p. 134. We are
indebted to Mr Jones for his assistance in providing
us with an advance copy of this article.

less discussed as a function of the law of blasphemy, but we mention it first since it is a view still undoubtedly held in some circles; indeed it seems to have been a factor influencing the institution of proceedings in Whitehouse v. Lemon.[309]

7.6   We do not think that the viewpoint under discussion can be a satisfactory rationale for the imposition of criminal penalties. Our correspondents who put forward this point of view did not indicate clearly what they considered the scope of legal sanctions ought to be, but many made reference to the importance to the well-being of the community in general in preserving and defending religious beliefs, and to what they considered to be displays of bad taste in the media. It therefore seems that ultimately those holding this point of view could be satisfied only by a very considerable broadening of the present bounds of the law of blasphemy. However this may be, the existence of this

---

309 The function of the offence in protecting beliefs per se was repeatedly emphasised in the summing-up and was explicit in the trial judge's comment on defence submissions: "You may think it is not a prosecution against the Christian religion, but rather ... a prosecution to protect the Christian religion": transcript of summing-up, p. 19. In Tracey and Morrison, Whitehouse (1979), p. 3, the prosecutor in the case is recorded as saying of her reaction to the poem by James Kirkup: "I don't think Jesus Christ has ever been more real to me as a person than he was at that particular moment. I felt I had to do something; I thought immediately of his crucifixion and of the way people turned and went away and left him, and I thought I would be like those if I did nothing ... So the only thing it seemed to me I could do at all was to see if it was blasphemous, if we could take action under the law". In the course of an interview shown on television on 16 March 1980 she stated "I did what I did in that case out of love of the Lord".

viewpoint clearly indicates that, for some, religion, religious institutions and belief in a Divinity are of fundamental importance; but we doubt if most people would regard this in itself as a reason for protection of these concepts by the criminal law. An instructive parallel may perhaps be drawn here with the influence upon the law formerly asserted by the Church in the field of family law. Whereas until the mid-19th century the matrimonial law of England and Wales remained in all essentials the canon law of the Church, the paths followed by the State and the Church have now diverged. The Church has abandoned the belief that its views in this sphere should dictate the secular law, for -

> "It has ... to be recognised that in a modern plural society the concept of human law is very different from that which obtained when the traditional theology of law was being formulated"

and

> "how the doctrine of Christ concerning marriage should be interpreted and applied within the Christian Church is one question: what the Church ought to say and do about secular laws of marriage and divorce is another question altogether."[310]

It may be thought that the viewpoint under discussion fails to take into account this change in the relationship between Church and State, and that from the standpoint of the criminal law it has lost its validity since blasphemy ceased to be regarded as an offence rooted in sedition.[311] Finally, it is worth noting that the

---

310 See Putting Asunder (1966), (Report of a Group appointed by the Archbishop of Canterbury in January 1964), paras. 6 and 15.

311 See paras. 2.3 and 2.13, above.

suggestion that the criminal law should intervene to
protect the Christian view of God, the Christian religion
or religious institutions appears to be incompatible
with the expressed desire of some proponents of criminal
sanctions to protect the beliefs of religions other than
Christianity. In our provisional view the argument
under consideration does not in contemporary circumstances
justify the imposition of criminal sanctions for
blasphemous conduct.

2.   The protection of society

7.7   The second argument in favour of criminal
sanctions relates to the effect that it is alleged
that blasphemy may have upon society as a whole, by virtue
of the unique position which religious beliefs hold among
a very substantial number, if not a majority, of the
people in this country. It is argued that vilifying
the sacred beliefs of a significant number of people -

> "can be more than a matter between
> the blasphemer and the insulted. It
> amounts to an attack on the fundamental
> decencies and mutual respect on which
> society operates, and could damage the
> stability of a community. Allowing
> total freedom to insult the religious
> beliefs of others can also have a
> profoundly adverse effect on the harmony
> that exists between different groups,
> particularly, perhaps, where racial
> and religious divisions go together."[312]

Furthermore, quite apart from considerations of public order,
the degree to which a society protects and upholds - even by

---

312   The Times (editorial), 13 July 1977.

the extreme sanction of the criminal law - the religious
beliefs of a substantial number of its members and the
ethical codes embodied in them is a real indication of the
state of civilisation of that society. In short, it is
argued that a law of blasphemy is needed -

> "to register the fact that there are certain
> things that are so repellent to the general
> conscience and mind of the country that this
> hostility to them should have some form of
> expression."[313]

It is apparent that "blasphemy" in the context of this
argument, and also of the next to be considered, includes
conduct of the type currently penalised by the common law,
that is, scurrilous or vilifying matter relating to
religion. The argument has powerful proponents and, if we
have understood it correctly, its acceptance as the
principal reason for criminal sanctions would justify
imposition of strict liability upon such conduct, because
it falls within the class of conduct which poses a threat
"to public health, public safety, public morals or public
order".[314]

7.8   This reasoning bears some resemblance to the
justification put forward by Lord Devlin for the
enforcement of morals by the criminal law.[315] But the

---

313   Hansard (H.L.) Vol. 389, col. 318, Bishop of
      Leicester. This is one example drawn from many in the
      debate on the Blasphemy Bill which maintained that
      the absence of criminal sanctions would endanger
      Christian standards of conduct and erode the values
      supporting society.

314   Whitehouse v. Lemon [1979] A.C. 617, 638 per Lord
      Diplock; see para. 2.21, above.

315   See Devlin The Enforcement of Morals (1965) and Hart
      Law, Liberty and Morality (1963). It should be noted
      that, although Lord Devlin stresses the interconnection
      of religion, morality and law, he nowhere suggests
      that the law should be used to protect religious
      beliefs.

debate as to the extent to which the law should act as a
custodian of public morality is one which we find it
unnecessary to explore. There is certainly room for the
argument that it is of fundamental importance to society
that religious beliefs should be treated with respect and
not subject to scurrilous comment. It can further be
argued that it is in the public interest that the feelings
of people in relation to matters which they hold sacred
should not be outraged, because of the distress which such
offensive attacks cause them. Such feelings would not be
outraged by rational and sober treatment of material, and
criminal sanctions would accordingly not attach to such
treatment. This may be regarded as the public aspect of
the argument which, in relation to the protection of the
individual, we examine below.[316] Countervailing
considerations, however, must in our view raise some doubt
as to whether these arguments are sufficiently strong on
their own to justify imposition of criminal sanctions.

7.9   Statements that what the law permits is the
"sober", "serious" or "rational" treatment of material, or
in particular "rational discussion" as distinct from
"scurrilous abuse", were commonplace in 19th century cases
and were echoed in Whitehouse v. Lemon.[317] But as both

---

316   See para. 7.12, below.

317   See the transcript of the trial judge's direction to
      the jury, pp. 3, 13 and 19, and [1979] A.C. 617, 662
      per Lord Scarman. And see the direction to the
      jury in R. v. Hetherington (para. 2.5, above) quoted
      by the trial judge, the Court of Appeal and the House
      of Lords in Whitehouse v. Lemon; also R. v. Ramsay
      and Foote (1883) 15 Cox C.C. 231, 239 per Coleridge
      L.C.J.

that and earlier cases clearly indicate,[318] it is quite
possible for a work of serious literature to induce outrage
among some people; and it is equally possible for rational
discussion, if it be sufficiently persuasive in setting
forth an unpopular argument, to induce a violently
unfavourable reaction. There is, however, a
counterbalancing public interest in ensuring that such
material is available to the public without the threat of
legal penalties. Moreover, the fact that such material may
induce outrage among some members of society raises the
question whether it is possible or practicable always to
distinguish sober, serious or rational material from
material which does not possess these characteristics. The
distinction assumes that it is possible always to separate
matter from manner, an assumption which may not be
well-founded:

> "The failing of the matter-manner distinction
> is that it supposes that statements are capable
> of more or less offensive formulations which
> are nevertheless identical in meaning. The
> manner of assertion is treated as though it were
> so much verbal wrapping paper whose features had
> no bearing upon the content of the parcel. In

---

318 In 1817 Shelley tried to regain custody of his children
after the death of his wife. Custody was refused by
Eldon L.C. after objection that he was an atheist who
had published a work ("Queen Mab") blasphemously
deriding the truth of the Christian revelation and
denying the existence of God as the creator of the
universe (Shelley v. Westbrooke (1817) Jac. 266, 37
E.R. 266; and see Jacob, Chancery Reports in the Time
of Eldon (1821) p. 266). In 1821 a bookseller, Clark,
was prosecuted by the Society for the Suppression of
Vice for selling the poem; he was convicted and
imprisoned. In 1841, while proceedings were pending
against him, Hetherington (see para. 2.5, above)
prosecuted a bookseller for selling Shelley's complete
works containing "Queen Mab"; he was convicted,
notwithstanding an eloquent defence which mentioned
writings alleged to be equally blasphemous by
Shakespeare, Milton, Byron and others (R. v. Moxon
(1841) St. Tr. N.S. 693). See Bonner, Penalties upon
Opinion (3rd ed., 1934) pp. 43 and 68, and Walter,
Blasphemy in Britain (1977) p. 3.

certain cases this assumption may not be
unjustified. By the insertion of a few
obscenities, a sentence can be rendered
more offensive while remaining virtually
unchanged in meaning. More often, however,
manner and matter are so integrally
related that it is impossible to
distinguish the offensive manner from the
offensive matter of a statement".[319]

In many instances, then, a distinction can be drawn between
matter and manner; but in some, material which is serious
or rational may nonetheless require the use of language
which is not "sober" in order fully to make its point and
which many may find offensive. This is well illustrated
by some of the material which in the past has been found
to be blasphemous. The passage which figured in R. v.
Bradlaugh, for example,[320] is doubtless highly coloured;
but the language does no more than lend point to what can now
be seen to be rational argument about the historical
nature of the Judaeo-Christian Deity. It was the argument
itself which was found unacceptable, no less than the
language in which it was couched. And while it may be
doubtful whether such writings would be found blasphemous
by a jury today, it may well be that attacks of this
nature upon the character of other religions would be found

---

319 Jones, "Blasphemy, Offensiveness and Law", (1980)
    B.J. Pol. S. 10, p. 129 at p. 143.

320 See (1883) 15 Cox C.C. 217 at p. 219; the passage
    reads: "The God whom Christians love and adore is
    depicted in the Bible with a character more blood-
    thirsty than a Bengal tiger or a Bashi-Bazouk. He is
    credited with all the vices and scarcely any of the
    virtues of a painted savage. Wanton cruelty and
    heartless barbarity are his essential characteristics.
    If any despot at the present time tried to emulate,
    at the expense of his subjects, the misdeeds of
    Jehovah, the great majority of Christian men would
    denounce his conduct in terms of indignation". The
    case was reported before the Law of Libel Amendment
    Act 1888, s. 3 of which now forbids the reporting
    of the libel: see para. 3.7, above.

quite unacceptable to their adherents. Yet if even this kind of material is to be exempt from criminal penalty because, despite its offensive character, it embodies rational argument and discussion, little appears to be left within the category of prohibited material save that which has no other purpose than to insult religious beliefs. Such publications may upon examination prove to be very few; but unless the scope of any offence were limited in this way, it might well be that freedom of expression would be subject to unacceptable constraints.[321]

7.10   Leaving aside the foregoing considerations, there remains the assertion that it is fundamental to society that religious beliefs should be treated with respect rather than scurrilously, and that failure to do so may have the adverse consequences against which proponents of this argument have warned.[322] It seems to us that assertions of this kind necessarily entail the further proposition that maintenance of respect for religious beliefs is as important to society as (according to one view) a shared morality,[323] and that without it society will suffer. If that is right, however, it seems to us to throw some doubt upon the validity of the distinction between the sober, serious and rational treatment of material and matter which is purely insulting. If society would indeed suffer as a result of an absence of respect shown to religious beliefs, it may be suggested that it will suffer all the more if such beliefs are subject to destructive analysis and criticism, even if temperately expressed, since reasoned persuasion is ultimately far more effective in its aim than attacks devoid of intellectual content. Yet it is precisely this type of publication

---

321   See further on this aspect, "Intention to Blaspheme", (1979) 129 New L.J. at p. 206.

322   See para. 7.7 and n. 313, above.

323   See para. 7.8 and n. 315, above.

which proponents of this argument are prepared to except from the ambit of criminal sanctions. Furthermore, it is in our view open to doubt whether the criminal law is an appropriate means of enforcing respect for religious beliefs, or whether, indeed, it is capable of doing so without resort to measures which would be regarded as unacceptable infringements upon freedom of expression in modern society. Such measures, it seems to us, could give rise to greater problems than they solve.[324]

7.11   We have indicated that to those who are profoundly convinced that blasphemous conduct is reprehensible and morally wrong, utilitarian arguments such as we have presented in the foregoing paragraphs will seem inadequate or unsatisfactory. But while recognising the powerful support which exists for the argument that criminal sanctions upon blasphemous conduct are necessary for the good of society as a whole, our examination of the argument suggests that it gives inadequate weight to the claims of freedom of expression, and that it has other serious weaknesses which militate against the imposition of criminal sanctions on this basis.

3.   The protection of individual feelings

7.12   The third, and in our view the most powerful, argument in favour of criminal sanctions is the effect which it is alleged that insults to religious belief may have on those holding such beliefs. The criminal law, it is suggested, should offer some protection to believers from suffering offence to their feelings. In other spheres the purpose, or at any rate one of the purposes, of the criminal law is to protect members of the public from offence or outrage; this is the case in such diverse

---

324 See further para. 7.17, below.

areas as offences which penalise indecent exposure and
other public sexual activities, or public nuisance which
penalises activities causing the emission of objectionable
noise and smells. Here the activity penalised consists of
conduct, whereas in the area of publications there is a
countervailing interest in freedom of expression which
will often outweigh the need to protect feelings from
offence: printed descriptions of such conduct are not, or
not necessarily, subject to penalties.[325] Nevertheless it
may be argued that the degree of offence caused by
blasphemous attacks may be so great as to cause serious
mental distress and should accordingly be subject to
penalties:

> "Blasphemy is an act of violence to the
> mind and spirit and deeply spiritual
> feelings of very large numbers, millions
> and millions, of people capable of
> entertaining such feelings. It is an
> assault upon the mind and spirit just as
> much as mayhem is an assault upon the
> body."[326]

And the "people capable of entertaining such feelings" are
not necessarily the minority who are practising and devout
Christians:

> "the relevant number in the context is not
> the number of churchgoers but the number of
> those who try, however feebly, to hold on to

---

325 See Jones, "Blasphemy, Offensiveness and Law" (1980)
B.J. Pol. S. 10, pp. 135 et seq. where the
appropriateness of the law to punish conduct which
causes offence is discussed at length. See also
Report on Conspiracy and Criminal Law Reform (1976)
Law Com. No. 76, paras. 3.107 et seq. and the
Criminal Law Revision Committee's Working Paper on
Sexual Offences (October 1980) paras. 136 et seq. in
regard to the need for an offence penalising sexual
conduct in public which may cause offence.

326 Hansard, (H.L.), 1978 Vol. 389, col. 290, Earl of
Halsbury.

Christian values and who want, however
seldom, to express these in a valid
Christian currency. This, I suggest, is
a very large number of people indeed,
well over half the population of this
country".327

7.13   While this reasoning suggests imposition of
criminal sanctions irrespective of the general criterion of
preserving public order, proponents of this argument
maintain that this would not amount to privileged treatment
of religion, for there are other areas in which the law
intervenes to limit freedom of speech regardless of
considerations of public order. Evidence for this is in
their view provided by section 5A of the Public Order Act
1936 which penalises public utterances likely to stir up
racial hatred.328   In this offence and in its predecessor
(section 6 of the Race Relations Act 1965) the emphasis has
shifted from the likelihood of the offending conduct causing
a breach of the peace (as in section 5 of the 1936 Act)329
towards the offensiveness of what is said, irrespective of
the manner in which it is expressed. Clearly (it is argued)
Parliament has taken the view that the laws for maintenance
of public order are insufficient to achieve the desired
social purpose in this area; thus it is open to Parliament
to take the same view in regard to protection of individuals'
religious beliefs.

7.14   The fundamental conflict of values between
proponents and opponents of criminal sanctions to which we
have already referred is particularly difficult to resolve
satisfactorily in this context. From the point of view
of opponents of criminal sanctions the question which this
argument raises is why freedom of speech should be

_____

327   Hansard, ibid., col. 304, the Bishop of Durham.
328   See para. 5.9, above.
329   See para. 5.6, above.

curtailed because a particular publication is thought to be grossly insulting to the feelings of others. The arguments for the intervention of the law assume a pre-eminent position for religious beliefs in the values of contemporary society which many opponents of criminal sanctions would not accept. If the religious beliefs of one part of the population require this protection, why should not the political beliefs of others be similarly protected? Or indeed the strongly held views of any section of the population upon any subject, such as the Monarchy or the flag? We think that the distinction between religious and other beliefs is most convincingly made in terms of the sacred nature of the former:

> "It is the special reverence felt for what
> is deemed sacred that makes people more
> susceptible to offence in relation to
> their religious beliefs than in relation
> to their political beliefs even though
> their political convictions may be no
> less strong. Ribald, obscene or abusive
> attacks upon God or Christ are the verbal
> equivalents of acts of desecration....
> For the religious adherent, the sacred is
> identified primarily as the divine or what
> is especially associated with the divine
> and only incidentally in terms of his
> feelings towards it."[330]

If this emphasis on the "special reverence felt for what is deemed sacred" rightly encapsulates the essential difference of outlook between proponents and opponents of criminal sanctions, as we believe it does, further comment is needed.

7.15   We think that opponents of criminal sanctions would concede that where overwhelming social pressures

---

330 Jones, "Blasphemy, Offensiveness and Law" (1980) B.J.
     Pol. S. 10, p. 138. See also C.L. Ten, "Blasphemy
     and Obscenity", (1978) Br. Jo. of Law and Society,
     Vol. 5, No. 1, p. 89; "Intention to Blaspheme"
     (1979) 129 New L.J. p. 205.

make it necessary, the general presumption in favour of freedom of speech both as to matter and manner may require modification either for the benefit of particular members of society or for the benefit of society as a whole. Such a course may be thought legitimate where the existing laws relating to security and public order have demonstrated their inadequacy, and where, in the absence of checks, the freedom to attack others by publication may lead to damage in terms of, for example, reputation or economic loss; here the law of civil defamation intervenes. And the special and pressing problem of racial discrimination led to the provisions in the Race Relations Acts 1965 and 1976, in order to help overcome the peculiar threat to the immigrant population which Parliament identified. The example of these provisions has, as we have noted, been urged by the proponents of criminal sanctions as a precedent for an offence in this area. But it may be thought that this comparison is not altogether convincing. There have indeed been instances of legislation exempting holders of particular religious beliefs from compliance with the general law.[331] But it does not follow that some members of society have been subjected to something approaching the same difficulties, pressures or attacks in respect of their religious beliefs as others have been on account of their race, and that those beliefs should therefore be protected in a similar manner. We incline to the view that the case for control of expressions of hostility towards religious beliefs by the criminal law gains support from the race relations legislation only if it can be demonstrated that

---

331   E.g., Shops Act 1950, s. 53 permitting occupiers of shops who observe the Jewish Sabbath to trade on Sundays; and the Motor-Cycle Crash-Helmets (Religious Exemption) Act 1976 which amends s. 32 of the Road Traffic Act 1972 to exempt Sikhs wearing turbans from being required by law to wear motor-cycle crash helmets.

there is a degree of hostility towards such beliefs
similar to that which prompted that legislation. In
fact there does not seem to us to be any genuine ground
for accepting the proposition that religious beliefs are
under threat or subject to overt hostility of the kind
or to the extent which necessitated the protection afforded
to ethnic minorities by section 5A of the Public Order Act
1936. Indeed, that section has a relevance to the laws
of blasphemy perhaps not appreciated by those who invoke
it as a precedent; for it suggests that, leaving aside
the general laws relating to public order and obscenity,
it is only in the most exceptional circumstances where
particular social tensions are in issue that the criminal
law ought properly to intervene to control the written
or spoken word. As we have noted,[332] it was the
importation of revolutionary and anti-clerical ideas in
the late 18th and early 19th century which at that time
gave rise to frequent prosecutions for blasphemous libel
because of the fear that the dissemination of such ideas
endangered the stability of society. By contrast, today
it is the large-scale immigration of post-War years which,
it may be argued, has engendered fears for that stability;
hence the wholly exceptional remedy in the criminal law
represented by the section of the Public Order Act 1936
(inserted by the Race Relations Act 1976) which penalises
incitement to racial hatred.

7.16   Yet even if the parallel with the Race
Relations Act must, as we suggest, be rejected, this does
not affect the fundamental argument that the particular
characteristic of "reverence felt for what is deemed
sacred"[333] may be thought to justify special protection

---

332 See para. 2.3, above.
333 See para. 7.14, above.

for the feelings of religious believers. But this argument
may itself not be sufficient if it can be demonstrated
that there are matters upon which others feel as strongly
and with as deeply-rooted conviction as the religious
believer. Where in a "plural society" there are strong
feelings over certain political and social ideals or over
the desecration of the national flag[334] and its
appropriation as an emblem by political fanatics - where,
in brief, these ideals and objects are regarded by
some as "sacred" - it may be thought that the feelings of
all such groups within society should be given no less
consideration than the feelings of the religious believer.
At best, then, it is arguable that "the sacred provides
some rationale for singling out religious feelings but
that rationale is one of degree."[335] If this is so, it
becomes more difficult to accept that there should be
special provision for the protection of the feelings of
the religious believer without affording equivalent
protection to other groups in society, for the most fervent
beliefs of these groups may at present be subject to any
kind of attack without interference from the law save in
matters of public order, obscenity and defamation of
character. On the other hand, this line of reasoning
assumes that religious feelings are not unique in
character, and although for some Marxists the philosophy
of dialectical materialism provides a faith which in many
respects possesses characteristics in common with some
major religions,[336] many religious believers may not be

---

334 A criminal offence in many countries and expressly
     provided for in section 250.9 of the American Law
     Institute's Model Penal Code (1962).

335 Jones, loc. cit., p. 138.

336 See Zaehner, "Dialectical Materialism" in Living
     Faiths (1977) pp. 393 et seq, especially at p. 397
     where Buddhism as the intellectual precursor of
     dialectical materialism is examined.

prepared to accept the general equivalence of political
ideals and religious beliefs. This does of course raise
difficult questions as to the nature of religious belief,
which we do not find it necessary to explore.[337] In any
event we cannot assume the argument outlined in this
paragraph to be acceptable to all members of society.
Furthermore, if it is possible to isolate material which
can be said to serve no real function but to insult the
religious feelings of others,[338] the countervailing argument
which stresses the paramount importance of freedom of
speech becomes less attractive; for the freedom to publish
material which serves that purpose only, and is therefore
designed gratuitously to wound the susceptibilities of
others, is, it seems to us, not an ideal which many would
be prepared to defend.

7.17   There are, however, other utilitarian arguments
which suggest that special legal protection for the
feelings of the religious believer is more difficult to
justify. It has been suggested to us that provision of
legal sanctions against matter designed to insult the
religious believer would indicate clearly the dividing
line between acceptable and unacceptable conduct. On the
other hand, it is arguable that special protection for the
religious believer could lead to widespread flouting of
legal sanctions by those wishing to focus attention upon its
discriminatory character or to be seen as martyrs in
the cause of freedom of expression. We have suggested that
it is difficult to maintain that a true parallel exists
between section 5A of the Public Order Act 1936, which
penalises incitement to racial hatred, and legal sanctions
against insults to religious feelings. Where, as in the
case of religious beliefs, little social need of this kind

---

337 But see para. 8.18, below.
338 As to whether this is possible, see para. 7.9, above.

for legal sanctions could be demonstrated, a law which was seen to be discriminatory in this sense might well stimulate activities designed to display its unacceptable character and the impossibility of securing its proper enforcement.[339] We believe that if this occurred, there would be a substantial risk that the law would thereby be brought into disrepute and at the same time be instrumental in creating a social problem where none at present exists.

7.18   It seems to us that the argument relating to protection of feelings also encounters considerable difficulties when an attempt is made to answer the question, "protection against what?" We deal in more detail with this below.[340] In the present context, it is relevant to note that the law currently penalises matter which is "scurrilous", or "abusive" or which "vilifies" Christ or the Christian religion.[341] We have some difficulty in discerning what conduct these words cover which is not already covered by other offences. The only recent precedent, the poem which figured in the prosecution in Whitehouse v. Lemon,[342] is of no assistance here: as the defence admitted,[343] proceedings against the publisher of the poem might in any event have been instituted under the

---

339 In this connection, it is relevant to note, first, the widespread publication and circulation of the poem figuring in Whitehouse v. Lemon after the prosecution in that case, and secondly, the publication shortly after the trial of Lemon of an illustrated book of "blasphemous" verse entitled "Good God". This is noted in Leigh, "Not to Judge but to Save" (1978) Cambrian L.J., p. 56, where the writer remarks that "it is a curious thing that the barring of a commodity may only serve to create a market for it."

340 See para. 8.7, below.

341 See para. 3.1, above.

342 [1979] A.C. 617.

343 See para. 5.3, above.

obscenity legislation; and it also seems likely that the
result of that case hinged to a considerable extent upon
the special meaning given by the trial judge to a "tendency
to a breach of the peace."[344] We think it right that, if
for example the poem in question were to be pinned up in a
convent, or if an attack upon Islam were to be displayed
in a mosque, such conduct overtly designed to attack the
feelings of people present in these places should
constitute some punishable offence. But rather than
provide an offence which would apply in all public places,
with its consequent restrictions upon freedom of
expression, we think it would be preferable to deal with
objectionable conduct of this kind in the context of
offences against religious worship; indeed, we
provisionally propose an offence penalising insulting
behaviour in places of worship in Part XII of this Working
Paper. The replies to our preliminary consultation
provide little or no guidance as to the nature of the
interest which the law should protect since, as we have
noted,[345] many of them contemplate a much wider legal
sanction. Their complaints relating to the media indicate
that the public dissemination of the incidental
profanities of ordinary speech into people's homes are
considered as objectionable as the material at which the
existing law of blasphemy is aimed. However, such conduct
cannot realistically be regarded as falling within the
scope of the law of blasphemy, and in any event a very
strong case would be required before concluding that
freedom of expression should be circumscribed to this
extent by the criminal law.

7.19   Two of the points made in preceding paragraphs -
the absence of social need, and the difficulty in defining
the matter against which protection might legitimately be

---

344 See paras. 2.15, 3.3 and 6.2, above.
345 See para. 7.2, above.

afforded - are both relevant to a further factor which may
be thought to weigh against the argument that the feelings
of religious believers deserve special protection.
Although the only recent case of blasphemy might have been
dealt with under the Obscene Publications Act 1959, it may
nonetheless be objected that any such proceedings would
have been unsuccessful because of the shortcomings in the
operation of that legislation which have led to recent
proposals for its reform.[346] But these proposals have
concentrated largely (although not exclusively) upon the
question of public display of indecent or offensive
material. As we have noted, the Williams Committee
recommendations would restrict the availability of
offensive pictorial material and ban its display.[347] The
Indecent Displays (Control) Bill recently debated in
Parliament would make it an offence publicly to display
any indecent matter.[348] The Williams Committee
recommendations would replace the Obscene Publications Act
1959, while the Indecent Displays (Control) Bill would
leave it untouched. These reforms concentrate upon the
public display of material because in the fields which
they cover such displays are currently regarded as a
significant social problem for which a workable remedy is
needed. There may also be publications available which

---

346 See para. 7.1, above.

347 See para. 5.4, above.

348 Under the Bill matter is publicly displayed if it is
     displayed in or so as to be visible from any public
     place, that is, any place to which the public have
     or are permitted to have access (whether on payment
     or otherwise) while the matter is displayed, except
     (a) a place to which the public are permitted to
     have access only on payment, including payment for
     the display, or (b) a shop or part of a shop to which
     the public can only gain access by passing beyond an
     adequate warning notice. In addition, to fall within
     these exceptions, persons under 18 must be excluded
     while the display is continuing.

could cause grave offence to the feelings of some
religious believers; but so far as we are aware, there is
little or no evidence that such material is forced upon
the gaze of an unwilling public, as is arguably the case
with indecent or pornographic matter. There remains a
high degree of choice on the part of the public as to
whether it should be made aware of such publications and
their contents. The very fact that members of society
retain such a degree of choice in our view tends to
strengthen the arguments set out in the preceding
paragraphs.

7.20   Before summing up our provisional views upon
the question whether legal sanctions are required for the
protection of the feelings of religious believers it is
right that we should note the views on that issue
expressed by Lord Scarman in Whitehouse v. Lemon, and in
particular his assertion[349] that -

> "in an increasingly plural society such as
> that of modern Britain it is necessary not
> only to respect the differing religious
> beliefs, feelings and practices of all but
> also to protect them from scurrility,
> vilification, ridicule and contempt."

It is undoubtedly the case that in consequence of the
growth of a multi-racial society, problems have been
encountered in the context of race, arising in part as a
result of competition for housing and employment and in
part from the everyday experience of living, travelling
and working alongside others who are different in
appearance, culture and perhaps language. These are
manifestations of distinctions which inherently have a
public aspect, and the law has been obliged to intervene.
But similar problems seem for the most part to have been
avoided in the context of religion. One reason for this

---

349   See [1979] A.C. 617 at p. 658, and also paras. 3.1
      and 6.9, above.

is that many ethnic immigrants, particularly those from the West Indies, share the same religion as the majority of religious believers in England and Wales. But the most important reason is that differences of religion impinge far less on the public eye: although it is possible that the position may change in the future, the practice of a particular faith is, save where religion and politics are inextricably mixed, a private matter giving rise to few opportunities for public friction. So far as England and Wales is concerned, it therefore does not seem to us to follow that the existence of a multi-racial society for that reason requires the provision of a law of blasphemy protecting a multiplicity of faiths. And where attacks on persons on account of their religion are in substance designed to stir up racial hatred, the law already makes provision.[350] So far as other parts of "modern Britain" are concerned, it has been observed that there may now be no law of blasphemy at all in Scotland;[351] and in Northern Ireland the law of blasphemy appears to play little, if any, role, even though it is the one part of the United Kingdom having a "plural society" with divided religious loyalties, where sectarian attacks are not

---

350 See para. 5.11, above, as to the position of Jews and the Jewish religion under s. 5A of the Public Order Act 1936, and for the view that s. 5 of the 1936 Act can be used to penalise insulting attacks on religious beliefs. Under s. 25(1) of the Race Relations Act 1971 (N.Z.) (similar to s. 6(1) of the Race Relations Act 1965, see para. 5.10, above) the New Zealand Court of Appeal has upheld the conviction of an accused for printing and publishing anti-semitic literature; Jews were held to have "ethnic origins" within the terms of that section. See Hodge, "Incitement to Racial Disharmony: King-Ansell v. Police" (1980) N.Z.L.J. p. 187. The case arose before the recent enactment of a provision similar to s. 5A, the Human Rights Commission Act 1977, s. 9A (N.Z.).

351 See para. 4.2, above.

uncommon.[352]

7.21   In examining the argument that a law of blasphemy
is required for protection against wounded feelings, we
have pointed out that the "special reverence for what is
deemed sacred" makes some individuals more susceptible to
offence in respect of their religious beliefs than any
other matter. It is, in our view, the unique character of
feelings in relation to religious beliefs which best
justifies special treatment by the law of attacks on them.
We do not think that the case for such special treatment
is strengthened by analogies with race relations
legislation, where the social issues appear to us to be
different. Furthermore, there are a number of
countervailing considerations which many may consider to
outweigh the need to accord special protection to religious
susceptibilities. Nevertheless, we consider that the
special feelings which many people undoubtedly have in
regard to religious beliefs is a factor which must be
taken into account in the ultimate decision as to whether
the criminal law should deal with blasphemous conduct as
such.

---

352   See para. 4.4, above. It is also worth noting that
      Lord Scarman quoted at length from Lord Sumner's
      speech in Bowman v. Secular Society Ltd. [1917] A.C.
      417 at pp. 466-467 (part of the relevant quotation
      appears in para. 2.13, above) in support of his view
      that the law of blasphemy should be adapted to suit
      what he saw as the "social conditions of the late 20th
      century" by widening its range of application: see
      Whitehouse v. Lemon [1979] A.C. 617 at p. 659. But it
      is clear that Lord Sumner was concerned to indicate
      that in the society of his time the scope of blasphemy
      was bound to be more limited. The relevant sentence
      from Lord Sumner's speech (at p. 467) reads:
      "experience having proved dangers once thought real to
      be now negligible and dangers once very possibly
      imminent to have now passed away, there is nothing in
      the general rules as to blasphemy and irreligion, as
      known to the law, which prevents us from varying their
      application to the particular circumstances of our
      time in accordance with that experience".

4. The protection of public order

7.22   Earlier in this Paper[353] we observed that, while some instances of blasphemous conduct could be dealt with by section 5 of the Public Order Act 1936, there were others which probably could not. In particular, section 5 requires that material be distributed or displayed and must at least be likely to occasion a breach of the peace. Thus it may not penalise the sale in a shop of printed matter which is not on its face abusive or insulting in relation to the Christian religion, but which does contain material that upon examination could prove to be of this character, and could therefore lead to a breach of the peace through individual or collective premeditated action at some time after the sale. No offence apart from blasphemous libel covers this situation, and in the final part of this section examining the justification for legal sanctions on blasphemous conduct, we consider whether this potential gap in the law is so significant as to warrant special provisions to deal with it.

7.23   The fact that blasphemy is capable of penalising certain publications which could lead to a breach of the peace as a result of later premeditated action, whereas section 5 of the Public Order Act probably does not, raises the issue, not merely whether there is a need to deal with this in the context of blasphemy, but whether the criminal law should penalise all publications which could conceivably lead to disorder. Generally speaking, the criminal law penalises publications which might lead to civil disorder only if they are a direct incitement to do so, in which case they either involve incitement to commit offences such as riot or affray, or indeed abusive and insulting behaviour under section 5, or

---

353 See paras. 5.6-5.8, above.

they constitute seditious libels. The one clear exception
in which publication is penalised where there is no
criterion of an immediate likelihood of the breach of the
peace[354] is section 5A of the Public Order Act 1936,
inserted by the Race Relations Act 1976,[355] where the
emphasis shifted from the consequences of publication in
terms of a breach of the peace to the content and
offensiveness of what is published. If this is the general
policy of the law, is there something so exceptionally
dangerous in insulting attacks on religion or religious
beliefs as to make it plausible in modern conditions that
breaches of the peace are a likely consequence of
publication, as distinct from the display or distribution
already dealt with by section 5 of the Public Order Act?
To justify on these grounds an offence penalising such
attacks, we think that it would have to be demonstrated
that there is, for example, a greater danger from this type
of publication than the publication and sale of extremist
political material. For reasons which we have already set
out,[356] we do not consider that any useful analogy can be
drawn with section 5A of the Public Order Act. Our
provisional view is that in modern conditions there is no
real likelihood of public disorder arising from publications
about religious matters, in whatever terms they are couched;
certainly no greater likelihood than arises from
publication of extremist political literature which,
subject to the general laws referred to above, is not in
any way penalised by the criminal law. If that is right,
it seems that reasons of public order are not sufficiently
strong in this field to warrant curbs upon freedom of
publication, and that existing offences in the public order

---

354 There is also criminal libel, but like seditious
     libel, this is being examined by us elsewhere: see
     para. 1.3, n. 2, above.

355 See para. 5.9, above.

356 See para. 7.15, above.

field are adequate to deal with any situations likely to
arise in consequence of the publication of blasphemous
material.

C. Summary

7.24   The preceding paragraphs have reviewed the
arguments which may be advanced for the retention of
criminal sanctions to deal with blasphemous conduct. Of
these, we have indicated that in our view the strongest is
that which suggests that insulting attacks upon matters
held sacred by religious believers causes injury to their
feelings of a unique kind in respect of those matters,
against which the law should provide protection. We have
examined a number of reasons why the assertion that these
feelings are unique in character, and so in need of
protection, may not be acceptable to many others in whose
lives religion does not play a central role; and we are
fully aware of the countervailing emphasis which many will
place upon the primacy of freedom of expression.
Nevertheless, we think there is room for the view that, if
the predominant purpose of a publication is to insult the
feelings of believers, such infliction of gratuitous
suffering on certain members of society may be thought
sufficient to warrant imposition of criminal sanctions.
On the other hand, we have not been convinced that a real
social need has been demonstrated for the intervention of
the criminal law. Thus it seems to us that there is no
single consideration which can be said to tip the balance
of argument decisively either for or against the provision
of criminal penalties.

7.25   We invite comment upon the arguments considered
in this part of the Paper, and upon the view we have
expressed[357] that there is little evidence that production

---

357 See para. 7.19, above.

of material whose predominant purpose is to insult the
feelings of religious believers is at present a social
problem of any significance. In this context we are,
however, not concerned with matters of taste in public
life or in broadcasting, which has its own system of
control,[358] where we doubt if criminal offences have any
role to play.[359] Thus we do not think that evidence of
the type of material we have in mind can be provided by
publications (whether in the form of broadcasts,
television shows or films) which, although intended to
poke fun in the interests of entertainment, are not
intended to outrage religious sensibilities and would not
reasonably be regarded as doing so by most of the audiences
watching, listening or paying to see the material
concerned.[360] Nor do we have in mind attacks upon non-
Christian religions amounting to thinly-disguised racial
hostility, with which the law already deals. Least of all
are we concerned with the incidental use in the media or
in public life of what is in the dictionary rather than the
legal sense profane or blasphemous language.[361] Our concern
is with public insults intentionally aimed at religious
beliefs whose predominant purpose is to cause distress to

---

358 See para. 5.13, above.

359 See paras. 7.2, 7.6 and 7.18, above.

360 E.g., television shows such as "Bless me Father",
     entertainers such as Billy Connolly and Dave Allen,
     films such as "The Life of Brian", or radio
     programmes such as "The Jason Explanation of
     Religion".

361 See paras. 2.1 and 7.2, above.

believers in relation to their faith.[362]

7.26   In our view the arguments for and against the
provision of criminal penalties are so evenly balanced that,
before coming to a provisional conclusion, it is necessary
to examine the various ways in which an offence to replace
the common law might be defined. If in formulating the
elements of such an offence it is found difficult or
impossible to define them satisfactorily, then, taken with
the apparent absence of a pressing social need for an
offence, this must weigh against the creation of any
offence. Accordingly, we now examine the form which new
legislation might take.

VIII POSSIBLE NEW OFFENCES

8.1   In order to examine fully the implications of
new legislation in this field, we believe that reform of
the law can best be considered by taking a critical look at
several possible offences, any one of which might replace
the common law. But before considering these possibilities,
it is necessary first of all to decide what the new
legislation would be designed to do. In Part XII of this

---

362 Tracey and Morrison, Whitehouse (1979) pp. 110-114
     describe an instance of this occurring in September
     1972 during an episode of a popular television series,
     where comments by the author and principal actor
     involved "made it very clear that they ... saw it as
     a means of attacking established religion and religious
     beliefs, to which they were both vehemently opposed".
     The D.P.P. declined to prosecute the B.B.C. for
     blasphemy because it had already admitted that the
     offending passage should not have been shown and
     because "the extreme nature of the vilification,
     ridicule or irreverence which would at the present
     day have to be established" made it unlikely that a
     prosecution would succeed. As to the criteria
     currently applied to broadcasting, see para. 5.13,
     above.

Paper we provisionally propose the creation of a new offence penalising offensive behaviour in places of worship. However, in relation to conduct in public which in general takes place outside these premises, we suggested in our examination of the arguments for maintenance of criminal sanctions that the strongest was that which suggested that certain conduct may wound or outrage the feelings of religious believers. It seems to us that this must be of the essence of any offence designed to replace the present law, the accepted definition of which, as we have noted,[363] takes no account of the effect which the proscribed conduct might have. Accordingly, this consideration must be borne in mind in the examination of various possible offences which follows. There may be other forms of offence which we have not considered, and we welcome comments not only on the possible offences which we discuss, but also on any others which commentators may wish to suggest.

8.2   The three possible offences which in our view fall to be discussed are -

> A. An offence of publishing insulting matter
>   likely to provoke a breach of the peace
>   by outraging the religious convictions
>   of others.
>
> B. An offence of incitement to religious
>   hatred.
>
> C. An offence of publicly wounding or outraging
>   the feelings of religious believers.

These are examined in the following paragraphs.

---

363 See paras. 2.1 and 3.1, above.

A. Publishing insulting matter likely to
provoke a breach of the peace by outraging
the religious convictions of others

8.3   We have already noted[364] that in 1930 a
Blasphemy Laws (Amendment) Bill was introduced into the
House of Commons and approved after a debate on second
reading,[365] but was subsequently dropped by its sponsors
as a result of a number of amendments introduced during the
committee stage which drastically altered its contents.
One amendment introduced by the Government would have
made it an offence punishable by a £100 fine or
imprisonment to publish "any matter of so scurrilous a
character as to be calculated by outraging the religious
convictions of any person to provoke a breach of the
peace". The consent of the Attorney General (or Solicitor
General) would have been necessary before the institution
of proceedings. The Bill was withdrawn by its sponsors
because other amendments introduced in Committee had the
effect of preserving the common law.

8.4   We do not think that an offence of this
character would be appropriate. It should be noted that
it was last suggested some years before the Public Order
Act 1936 was enacted which, while it does not cover mere
"publication", provides in section 5 a wide offence
penalising display or distribution of insulting matter
likely to lead to a breach of the peace.[366] In our

---

364 See para. 2.25, above.

365 See Hansard H.C. (1930) Vol. 234, cols. 495-572;
     also H.B. Bonner, Penalties Upon Opinion (3rd ed.,
     1934) at pp. 130-132. Suggestions for a similar
     offence are made by Amphlett Micklewright,
     "Blasphemy and the Law" (1979) Law & Justice
     No. 60-61, p. 20 at p. 31.

366 See para. 5.6, above.

examination of the arguments in favour of criminal sanctions, we provisionally concluded that existing offences in the public order field, including section 5 of the 1936 Act, are adequate to deal with any situations likely to arise in consequence of the publication of blasphemous material, and that in modern conditions reasons of public order are not sufficiently strong to warrant further curbs on freedom of expression in this area.[367] Accordingly, we provisionally reject an offence cast in these terms.

B. Incitement to religious hatred

8.5   A second possibility is an offence of incitement to hatred of people on account of their religious beliefs. This would involve the addition of the words "or religious" after the word "racial" in section 5A (1) of the Public Order Act 1936;[368] the section would thereby penalise insulting behaviour -

> "in a case where, having regard to all the circumstances, hatred is likely to be stirred up against any racial or religious group ... by the matter or words in question".

We have noted that this suggestion was considered and rejected in 1965, when the section's predecessor was enacted.[369] We do not think that such an amendment would help in the present context. We have already stated that in our view there is no parallel in England and Wales between the social pressures on racial groups which gave rise to the necessity, as the Government saw it, of introducing section 5A, and the present situation in regard to religious worship.[370] There seems to us to be

367   See para. 7.23, above.
368   See para. 5.9, above.
369   See para. 5.11, above.
370   See para. 7.15, above.

little call for such an offence at present, and as we have pointed out, the creation of new offences of this kind for which there is no demonstrable need often focusses attention upon them and may even provoke unlooked-for trouble.[371] But the decisive argument against an offence of this character is that it would be concerned, not with protecting feelings of individuals wounded by insults relating to their religious beliefs, but with prevention of incitement to hatred of such individuals because they hold particular religious beliefs. This is something quite different, and although the amendment to the Race Relations Act outlined above could be made if in future stirring up hatred against people of a particular religion becomes a significant problem, provisionally we do not think that this would be an appropriate option in the present context.

C. Publicly insulting the feelings of religious believers

8.6 Unlike the two possible offences discussed above, there are no precedents in this country for an offence of which the essence is the act of wounding the feelings of particular groups of individuals by public insults of a particular character.[372] There are, however, precedents which may assist in isolating the elements of such an offence which will need discussion. In particular, we

---

371 See para. 7.17, above; see also the Prevention of Incitement to Hatred Act (Northern Ireland), 1970, noted in para. 5.12, above.

372 Criminal libel is concerned with damage to reputation rather than the act of wounding, section 5A of the Public Order Act 1936 (incitement to racial hatred) with the likely effect on persons incited rather than the effect on the racial groups concerned.

have noted the provision in the Indian Penal Code, which
was designed to cope with the problems of a society
divided in its religious beliefs.[373] We consider the
requisite elements in the following paragraphs.

1. The prohibited conduct

8.7   The first element to be considered is the
prohibited conduct (the actus reus) of the offence, which
we tentatively describe as the "publication of matter
which is likely to wound or outrage the feelings of the
adherents of a religion". Although we believe the terms
"wound or outrage" are probably the most apt in the
circumstances, we do not attach too much importance to
the precise wording here. This is because, whichever
words are used, it is plain that an offence described in
these terms alone is far too wide to stand on its own and
requires qualification. The range of topics which are
capable of causing offence to the feelings of any one of
the numerous religious groups in this country is so wide
that it would constitute an unprecedented curb on freedom
of speech.[374] It would, for instance, be capable of
outlawing any public discussion of artificial means of
birth control, the use of blood transfusions to save life
and, indeed, the use of drugs for medical treatment. In

---

373 See paras. 4.10-4.11, above; and see further
     para. 8.11, below.

374 See e.g. Professor Smith in [1979] Crim. L.R. at
     pp. 312-313 who, in commenting on Lord Scarman's
     obiter dicta in Whitehouse v. Lemon in favour of
     extending the law of blasphemy to other faiths
     (see paras. 6.9 and 7.20, above), suggests that
     "vilification, ridicule, and contempt may be
     decidedly in the public interest. Should it not be
     possible to attack in the strongest terms religious
     beliefs that adulterers should be stoned to death
     and that thieves should have the offending hand
     lopped off, however offensive that may be to the
     holders of the belief?".

fact, any statement contradicting the cherished doctrines of any one of the hundreds of sects practising in this country might be capable of becoming a criminal offence. It is only necessary to state this proposition to realise its absurdity. Our chief concern, then, must be the most appropriate means of qualifying the breadth of the actus reus.

8.8   Whichever course is adopted with this in mind seems to us to have drawbacks or to involve a degree of uncertainty. We have already stated why in our view it would not be satisfactory to limit the ambit of an offence merely by provision of consent to institution of proceedings.[375] The means adopted in the present law of blasphemy is the addition of any number of adjectives describing the published matter - "scurrilous", "ludicrous", "abusive", and the like[376] - which, in addition to their drawback of uncertainty,[377] have in the present context little purpose: if matter is indeed capable of wounding and outraging the feelings of religious believers, in principle it should be irrelevant (as it is in the Indian Code) whether the mode of expression is scurrilous or otherwise.[378] Descriptive words of this character are for these reasons inappropriate for legislation. There are, we think, two possible methods of limiting the prohibited conduct: the addition of a restrictive mental element, and (whether or not such an element is included) qualification of the actus reus by defences or restrictions. We examine these possibilities in the following paragraphs.

---

375   See para. 6.10, above.

376   See para. 3.1, above.

377   See para. 6.1, above.

378   Although the mode of expression may be highly relevant to proof of the mental element. As to whether it is possible to distinguish matter and manner, see para. 7.9, above.

2. Possible limitations on the prohibited conduct

8.9   The first possible provision in relation to the actus reus is a requirement that the publication must be shown to be offensive to the public at large, which would reflect the definition of "publication" proposed below.[379] But there are serious objections to such a provision. The general public may not be offended by attacks upon the feelings of the adherents of minority religions, and may indeed regard some attacks as justifiable comment.[380] A provision on these lines might therefore go far to eliminate any protection for such groups or sects. Furthermore it would be difficult to operate in practice without admitting evidence as to the state of public opinion on the point at issue. A more practicable alternative might be a requirement that the publication must be such that a reasonable man would appreciate its offensiveness in the circumstances of the case. This also has clear drawbacks. The jury would still be required to decide whether the publication in question wounded or outraged the feelings of religious believers. To require the jury in addition to answer the question whether, in effect, it found the publication offensive would render the offence as uncertain in scope as the present law, where the reliance upon descriptive words of this character is, as we noted in the preceding paragraph, a major disadvantage. Thus in our provisional view neither of these possible additional requirements is satisfactory.

---

379 See para. 8.14, below. And compare the recommendation of the Williams Committee Report on Obscenity and Film Censorship (1979) Cmnd. 7772 as to matter whose availability should be "restricted": see para. 5.4, above.

380 See para. 8.15 and n. 397, below.

8.10   Secondly, it would be possible to provide a
defence to enable a defendant to show that, if wounding
or outraging the feelings of others did result from the
publication in question, it was an ancillary effect
irrelevant to his objective in publishing, and that the
value of the publication in terms of that objective
outweighed its capacity to wound or outrage. We put
forward this defence only as a possibility, particularly
since the Williams Committee did not favour a defence of
"public good" in the context of the subject matter within
the scope of its review.[381] But such a provision may be
thought desirable having regard to the difficulty in
distinguishing in this context between, on the one hand,
a defendant's purpose or motive and, on the other, the
legal requirement of a mental element of intention,[382]
and the consequent need to provide some protection to
safeguard the scientist, artist, social critic or writer
whose work, or the publication of whose work, may have
the effect of wounding or outraging certain religious
sensibilities. While a defence of this character carries
with it the risk of more lengthy trials, some may take the
view that this is a risk which should be taken, having
regard to the potential effects of the offence upon
freedom of expression.

3. The mental element

8.11   Another means of restricting the ambit of the
actus reus is the provision of a restrictive mental element

---

381   See (1979) Cmnd. 7772, para. 9.41; in the context
      of obscene material the Committee thought a defence
      of artistic merit unworkable, and in any event the
      question did not arise in the case of literary works
      since restrictions under the Committee's
      recommendations would not apply to the written word:
      see para. 5.4, above.

382   See paras. 6.7-6.8, above.

requiring proof of intent to wound and outrage. This would involve a departure from the present law of blasphemy as determined in Whitehouse v. Lemon, but we agree with the minority in that case that any other course in modern conditions would be a retrograde step in the development of the criminal law.[383] It is true that, as we have shown,[384] the requirement of a mental element was eliminated from legislation penalising incitement to racial hatred; but that course was considered necessary in order to deal effectively with a pressing social problem which seems to us to have no parallel in the field of attacks on religious feelings.[385] Furthermore, we have seen that the provisions of the Indian Penal Code, expressly designed to cope with the problems of a society divided or "plural" in its religious beliefs, require a stringent mental element.[386] Even if belief in the basic tenets of Christianity is the predominant religious feeling in England and Wales, large numbers of people in society nonetheless hold a variety of religious beliefs or none at all; and it is correspondingly more difficult to ascertain in advance whether matter is capable of wounding feelings in regard to particular beliefs. Thus in our view a mental element of intent to wound such feelings is all the more necessary and desirable. And in this instance we consider it appropriate that "intent" should bear as restricted a meaning as possible: provisionally we suggest the exclusion here of the broader meaning of intent recommended in our Report on the Mental Element

---

383 See [1979] A.C. 617, 638 (Lord Diplock) and 656 (Lord Edmund-Davies); and see paras. 2.22 and 6.3, above, especially n. 271.

384 See para. 5.10, above.

385 See para. 7.15, above.

386 See paras. 4.10-4.11, above.

in Crime.[387] Furthermore, in our view the prosecution
should be required to prove participation in publication
according to the normal principles of criminal liability;
vicarious liability should not suffice, nor should a
defendant have the burden of proving lack of knowledge of,
or absence of negligence in relation to, publication
without his authority.[388]

8.12   If, contrary to our provisional view, it were
thought undesirable to make provision for a mental element
in any new statutory offence, we consider that the possible
offence under consideration would instead require stringent
limitations upon the element of "publication". These
would include -

> (a) A defence for distributors of newspapers,
> books etc. of lack of knowledge that the
> matter contained material liable to
> prosecution for the offence.

> (b) A defence for broadcasting authorities in
> respect of unforeseen blasphemous
> statements made during the course of live,
> unscripted broadcasts.[389]

---

387 (1978) Law Com. No. 89. In para. 44 we recommend
     that in future legislation "a person should be
     regarded as intending a particular result of his
     conduct if, but only if, either he actually intends
     that result or he has no substantial doubt that the
     conduct will have that result" (emphasis added).
     Thus in the present instance the second limb would
     be excluded.

388 Compare the Libel Act 1843, s. 7 and para. 3.6, above.
     And see Whitehouse v. Lemon [1979] A.C. 617, 656 per
     Lord Edmund-Davies, quoted in para. 6.8, above.

389 The Report of the Committee on Defamation (the Faulks
     Committee) rejected such a defence for civil libel:
     see (1975) Cmnd. 5909, paras. 299-300.

8.13   It will be apparent that in our provisional
view a stringent mental element should be a requirement
of the possible offence under consideration. We have
considerable doubts about the other limitations upon the
conduct to be penalised, which we have discussed in
paragraphs 8.9-8.10. While there may be arguments in
their favour, they might in practice prove unworkable. We
welcome comment upon this and on the other matters
discussed in the foregoing paragraphs. The other elements
of the proposed offence must now be considered.

4. Mode of publication

8.14   Publication is an essential element of the
possible offence under consideration. But should
publication in this context denote public display, or
public availability and distribution? At present the law
penalises the latter;[390] but we have noted that, in the
context of the law of obscenity, proposals for reform have
concentrated on the former.[391] However, we have also
noted[392] that there appears to be little evidence of public
display of matter which is offensive solely because it
wounds religious susceptibilities;[393] and if "publication"
were confined to public display, the offence could for
that reason seldom be invoked. In itself this may suggest
that there is no real need for it. In order to give a
possible content to an offence, we have concluded that the
appropriate definition of publication here is that used in
section 5A of the Public Order Act 1936 (incitement to

---

390 See para. 3.5, above.
391 See para. 7.19, above.
392 Ibid.
393 But as to such displays in places of worship, see
     para. 12.16, below.

racial hatred), that is, publication and distribution to the public at large. But unlike that provision, we do not think that publication should be confined to written matter: if there is to be an offence, we believe it should extend to publication by any means of communication, whether by radio, television or otherwise.

5. The meaning of "religion"

(a) The need for a definition

8.15   One of the principal anomalies of the present law of blasphemy is, as we have noted, the narrow scope of its protection, which does not extend beyond the Christian religion.[394] To which religions should the offence under discussion be restricted, and by what means? Much of the difficulty in this context would be eliminated by the requirement we have suggested that the publication in question must not only wound and outrage the feelings of a religious believer but must also be offensive to the public at large; it is unlikely that a publication directed at a religion with a small number of adherents would have this effect. If, however, this requirement was not an acceptable element of the offence, the question remains whether "religion" needs definition. It is not defined in civil law codes; but as we have pointed out,[395] their provisions do not have the precision which is generally thought desirable in criminal law statutes in this country. Nor is religion defined in the provisions of the Indian Penal Code;[396] but the presence of a

---

394 See paras. 3.2 and 6.9, above.
395 See paras. 4.12-4.13, above.
396 See paras. 4.10-4.11, above.

multiplicity of religions in our own society and the
desirability of taking account of other social factors
suggest that the solution provided by that Code would not
be appropriate in this country. In particular, there may
be instances where it is very much in the public interest
that the beliefs and practices of particular religious
sects should come under sharp criticism,[397] and in those
cases we think it would be inappropriate for the criminal
law to give even a semblance of protection to the feelings
of their adherents. Accordingly, we have examined several
possible definitions which we outline in the following
paragraphs.

(b) Limitation to Christianity

8.16   The first possibility is to adhere in this
respect to the existing law; the feelings of members of
the established Church would be protected, but not those
of other Christian churches. Although this is a simple
solution which was supported by a few of our correspondents,
we doubt if it would have widespread support today, and

---

397 See para. 8.7, n. 374, above. The possible social
     benefits of such attacks were recently pointed out in
     Attorney General v. B.B.C. [1980] 3 W.L.R. 109, where
     at p. 120 Lord Salmon said "The B.B.C.'s attack on
     September 26, 1976, if true, was a very real service
     to the public; it purported to expose the misery and
     harm caused by the Brethren to the many young people
     whom they enlisted and cruelly cut off from their
     mothers, fathers, brothers, sisters and friends, and
     indeed from anyone who had not joined the ranks of
     the Exclusive Brethren...." The practices of other
     sects have also been attacked in Parliament, where
     it has been alleged that "very undesirable means are
     used, especially by the 'Moonies', to capture the
     allegiance especially of young people and to retain
     it once they have initially succeeded" and that "many
     people believe that these organisations [the Church
     of Scientology and the Unification Church] are doing
     great mental harm to the young people whom they
     capture in this way" (Hansard (H.L.) 1980 Vol. 412,
     cols. 1766 and 1768, per the Bishop of London and
     Lord Orr-Ewing).

we could certainly not recommend it unless Church leaders lent it their support. The existing law of blasphemy is limited in this way for historical reasons to which we referred at the beginning of this Paper; but there seems to be no valid reason for so confining an offence which is concerned with the protection, not of the Church itself, but of the feelings of religious believers. Another possibility is to extend protection to adherents of all Christian churches in this country. Again, this has had the support of some of our correspondents because, however "plural" our society may be in many respects, fundamentally it remains a "Christian country" the great majority of whose population subscribes to Christian ethics and morality. On the other hand, even if this is conceded, it has to be borne in mind that the proposed offence is concerned, not with the protection of particular moral values, but with injury to the feelings of individuals. There are, as we point out below,[398] literally hundreds of Christian sects in this country, and it might be thought unacceptable today for the feelings of a sect having at most a few hundred adherents to be protected by law, but not those of adherents of non-Christian religions numbering hundreds of thousands.

(c) Extension to other religions

8.17   The extension of the offence to protect the feelings of adherents of religions generally could, it seems to us, be effected by one or other of two methods: the provision of some new, comprehensive definition, or the use of some existing criterion. Of these, the provision of an overall definition appears, on the examples we have considered, uniformly to have the drawback of insufficient certainty. This is undoubtedly the case with such commonly

---

398 See para. 8.20, below.

suggested criteria as "major" religions or religions "with
a substantial number of adherents", which in our view
would present courts with insoluble problems. It is
similarly the case with another suggestion,[399] to the
effect that a religion should not be protected if it holds
beliefs or practices contrary to public policy. Furthermore,
we do not think that the concept of "public policy" is one
which is appropriate for inclusion in a criminal offence.
Its purport may be obvious enough in the obvious case - as
instanced by the sect involved in the Jonesville mass
suicide - but, quite apart from its inherent uncertainty
of application, in other instances it may be a matter of
controversy as to whether practices are contrary to the
concept.

8.18   Various approaches towards a comprehensive
definition of religion or what is religious have been
advanced in other contexts, but none of these seem to us
appropriate for inclusion in legislation. Thus, as we note
below,[400] it has been necessary to consider the nature of
"religious worship" in the context of section 2 of the
Ecclesiastical Courts Jurisdiction Act 1860. Again, it
has recently been considered whether objects of a charity
were for the advancement of religion in a case where the
objects were "the study and dissemination of ethical
principles and the cultivation of a rational religious
sentiment";[401] but while illuminating this area of the
law, the decision suggested no definitions which would be

---

399 Amphlett Micklewright, "Blasphemy and the Law"
     (1979) Law & Justice No. 60 - 61, p. 20.

400 See para. 12.7, below and R. v. Registrar General
     Ex. p. Segerdal [1970] 2 Q.B. 697.

401 In re South Place Ethical Society, Barralet v.
     Attorney General [1980] 1 W.L.R. 1565.

helpful in the present context. Finally, we have noted[402] the development of the law in the United States in relation to the two clauses of the first amendment to the Constitution relating to religion.[403] In defining religion here, earlier Supreme Court cases stressed worship of a deity.[404] In the 1940's there began a shift of emphasis towards the relationship of man to the universe and to other men,[405] which by the 1960's led the court to identify as religious beliefs Secular Humanism and Ethical Culture, among others.[406] Two subsequent decisions made clear that religious beliefs include all sincere beliefs "based upon a power or being, or upon a faith, to which all else is subordinate or upon which all else is ultimately dependent",[407] and that purely ethical and moral considerations are religious.[408] We do not suggest that this development is of immediate value for present purposes; but it does suggest that any definition of religion which confines itself to, or is dependent on, the element of submission to or worship of a deity may ultimately prove inadequate to take account of changes in society.

---

402   See generally "Towards a Constitutional Definition of Religion" (1978) 91 Harv. L.R. 1056 (unsigned note).

403   "Congress shall make no law respecting an establishment of religion, or prohibiting the free exercise thereof ...".

404   E.g., "The term 'religion' has reference to one's views of his relations to his Creator, and to the obligations they impose of reverence for his being and character, and of obedience to his will": Davis v. Beason 133 U.S. 333 (1890), at p. 342.

405   See U.S. v. Kauten 133 F.2d 703 (2d Cir. 1943).

406   Torcaso v. Watkins 367 U.S. 488 (1961).

407   U.S. v. Seeger 380 U.S. 163 (1965); see In re South Place Ethical Society [1980] 1 W.L.R. 1565 at pp. 1570-71.

408   Welsh v. U.S. 398 U.S. 333 (1970). This and the preceding case concerned the interpretation of a statutory provision relating to conscientious objection to military service containing a requirement of belief "in a relation to a Supreme Being".

8.19   We now consider whether the range of religions outside Christianity may be identified by reference to some existing criterion. A suggestion made to us by one of our correspondents was that religion in this context should mean all theistic religious groups recognised by the Charity Commissioners. But we doubt whether it is realistic to define the scope of an essential element of a criminal offence by this means. The numbers of religions or sects would be extraordinarily large, including - as it would - missions led by individuals whose religious work has been held the valid object of a charitable gift.[409] Moreover, it might have results which some would find surprising.[410] In any event "the law as to religious charities is ... in the same unholy mess as that relating to other types of charity",[411] and the Charity Commissioners themselves have recently pointed out that it is a misconception "that the registration of an institution as a charity is ... evidence that ... the trustees and servants of the charity are of good character".[412]

---

409   See e.g. Re Watson, Hobbs v. Smith [1973] 1 W.L.R. 1472. Confining religions to those which are theistic might also exclue Buddhism, though certain Buddhists have said that they do not favour this kind of legal protection: see Sangharakshita (D.P.E. Lingwood), Buddhism and Blasphemy (1978); and see R. v. Registrar General, Ex p. Segerdal [1970] 2 Q.B. 697 at p. 707 (Lord Denning M.R.) and In re South Place Ethical Society [1980] 1 W.L.R. 1565 at p. 1573.

410   Thus on the issue of whether a charity is for the public benefit, compare Gilmour v. Coats [1949] A.C. 426 (bequest to enclosed Roman Catholic convent not charitable) and Holmes v. Attorney General, The Times 12 February 1981 (trust for benefit of the Exclusive Brethren held charitable).

411   Keeton and Sheridan, The Modern Law of Charities (2nd ed., 1971), p. 52.

412   Report of the Charity Commissioners for England and Wales (1975) paras. 87-94, commenting on the charities "all connected in some way with Mr R.C.A. Gleaves", whose activities were described in the book Johnny Go Home.

133

8.20   We have examined two further solutions to this problem by reference to existing criteria, but both have disadvantages of their own. The first would define "religions" by reference to those whose places of worship are certified by the Registrar General under the Places of Religious Worship Registration Act 1855, read with the Ecclesiastical Courts Jurisdiction Act 1860. These provisions are explained in detail in Part XII of this Paper.[413] However, this solution would present substantial difficulties. There is no comprehensive list publicly available of the religions whose places of worship are currently certified;[414] the criterion would not necessarily exclude the sects which in the public interest should be exposed to public scrutiny and criticism;[415] and from a list of religions whose places of worship have now or since 1855 been certified, supplied to us by the Registrar General's Office, it is evident that certification extends (or has extended) to some six hundred sects, many of them probably minuscule in the number of their adherents. Furthermore, although the criterion of certification is, as we explain below,[416] used for the purpose of defining the scope of the offence under section 2 of the Ecclesiastical Courts Jurisdiction Act 1860 of "riotous, violent or indecent behaviour" in any certified place of religious worship, it is questionable whether that criterion is appropriate for the very different offence of public statements affecting the feelings of religious believers.

---

413 See para. 12.6, below.

414 A register of all the places of worship in respect of which certificates have been given is open to public inspection.

415 See para. 12.7, below as to the criteria applied when effecting certification under the Places of Religious Worship Registration Act 1855.

416 Ibid.

8.21   The other possibility is to schedule the
religions to which the offence under consideration would
apply. But exclusion from any such schedule would
inevitably imply that the religions or sects concerned
were either unimportant, or worse still, considered by
Parliament to be in some way harmful. In our view,
therefore, such a listing could not avoid promoting
division in the community. Thus, of the possibilities
discussed in this and the preceding paragraph, a
definition of religion by reference to those whose places
of worship are certified by the Registrar General seems
to us marginally preferable. But the difficulties
attaching to it to which we have referred cannot in our
view make this by any means a satisfactory solution.

(d) Conclusion

8.22   Our survey of the possible means of defining
religion suggests that there are no satisfactory answers
for our purposes: each course has serious disadvantages.
In the context of the criminal law it seems to us
essential that it should be known in advance whose feelings
the proposed offence is intended to protect; this
requires a definition having a high degree of certainty.
Of those which we have examined, definition by reference
to a schedule of religions or by reference to those whose
places of worship are certified by the Registrar General
are both possibilities, with the last-mentioned being
perhaps less unsatisfactory. However, the absence of
any satisfactory definition clearly has important
implications, which we consider further below.[417] We
welcome comment upon the definitions which we have
discussed and invite further solutions to the problem.

---

417 See para. 9.2, below.

6. Procedure and penalties

8.23   We do not think that any new offence should
perpetuate the special procedure for institution of
blasphemy proceedings under the Law of Libel Amendment Act
1888.[418] It is, however, for consideration whether there
should be some kind of consent required for the institution
of proceedings. We have pointed out that such a requirement
cannot in our view cure substantive defects in the law.[419]
For that reason it would be unsatisfactory, for example,
to leave "religion" undefined and rely upon a consent
provision to cure the consequent uncertainty in the law.
But such a requirement is legitimate where it is desired to
take into account exceptional considerations of public
policy, to secure a greater than usual degree of uniformity
in the criteria adopted for prosecution, and to exclude
prosecution of trivial cases. We believe that, having
regard to the kind of offence which we have outlined, this
is an instance where the above-mentioned considerations
make it appropriate to provide for the consent of the
Attorney General or Director of Public Prosecutions to the
institution of proceedings. We invite the views of
commentators on this issue.

8.24   As regards mode of trial and penalties, it seems
to us that provision of a full mental element of intent to
wound and outrage the feelings of believers would make it
appropriate for the defendant to be given the opportunity
of giving evidence before a jury, but that the offence should
be considered less serious than the offence of incitement to
racial hatred under section 5A of the Public Order Act 1936.
Our provisional proposal is, therefore, that if there is to
be an offence, it should be triable either way (that is,

---

418 See para. 3.7, above.
419 See para. 6.10, above.

either on indictment or summarily in a magistrates' court) with a maximum penalty on indictment of 12 months' imprisonment and a fine.[420]

7. Summary

8.25   If it is thought that there is a need for an offence in place of the common law, we put forward for consideration and comment a new offence which would have the following elements -

> (a) Publishing matter which is likely to wound or outrage the feelings of the adherents of any religious group, with intent to do so.

> (b) "Publication" should mean publication or distribution to the public at large and should extend to any means of communication, whether by radio, television or otherwise.

> (c) "Religious group" should be defined. There seems to be no entirely acceptable method of doing this, but there are two possibilities:

>> - defining such groups by reference to those whose places of worship are certified under the Places of Religious Worship Registration Act 1855, or

>> - listing all the religious groups to which the offence should apply.

---

420   This was the maximum provided for the Public Order Act 1936, s. 5 under the Public Order Act 1963, but under the Criminal Law Act 1977 this offence became triable summarily only: see para. 5.6, above.

Tentatively, the first seems less
unsatisfactory.

(d) The offence should be triable either
way with a maximum penalty on indictment
of 12 months' imprisonment and a fine.

(e) The consent of the Attorney General or
Director of Public Prosecutions should
be required for the institution of
proceedings.

If, contrary to our view, it was thought undesirable to have
the mental element prescribed in (a) by the words "with
intent to do so", it would be necessary to provide in
addition -

(f) A defence for distributors of lack of
knowledge that the matter contained
material liable to prosecution for the
offence, and a defence for broadcasting
authorities in respect of unforeseen
blasphemous statements made during the
course of live, unscripted broadcasts.

It is for consideration whether the conduct to be penalised
summarised in (a), above (whether with or without the words
"with intent to do so") should be restricted by additional
provisions -

(g) A requirement that the publication must
be such that a reasonable man would
appreciate its offensiveness in the
circumstances of the case, or alternatively
that the publication must be shown to be
offensive to the public at large.

(h)   A defence enabling a defendant to show
        that if wounding or outraging the
        feelings of others did result from
        publication, it was an ancillary
        effect irrelevant to his objective in
        publishing, and that the value of the
        publication in terms of that objective
        outweighed its capacity to wound or
        outrage.

Neither (g) nor (h) would be satisfactory.

IX   PROVISIONAL CONCLUSION

9.1   Earlier in this Paper[421] we indicated that in
our view the range and strength of arguments for and against
the provision of criminal penalties upon blasphemous conduct
were evenly balanced. On the one hand, there seems to us
no evidence of particular social tensions or of attacks
upon religious beliefs which demand that this conduct be
subject to the criminal law, and the requirements of public
order are adequately met by the present law. Moreover,
there is a wide range of other offences capable of dealing
with some kinds of blasphemous conduct, and the imposition
of any further penalties might involve unacceptable
restrictions upon freedom of expression. On the other hand,
these utilitarian arguments could not be expected to
satisfy those for whom blasphemous conduct is so
reprehensible and morally wrong that the law ought to
intervene. Furthermore, feelings in regard to the religious
and the sacred are arguably unique in character and on that
account require some special protection by the law against
attacks causing serious suffering.

---

421 See para. 7.26, above.

9.2   Since the arguments were evenly balanced, we decided to examine the form which a possible new offence might take before coming to a provisional conclusion. We considered that the most appropriate kind of offence would be one which penalised publication of matter which is likely to wound or outrage the feelings of the adherents of any religious group, with intent to do so. There is, however, some difficulty in framing the conduct to be penalised in a suitably restricted way which will not involve the risk of undue limitations upon freedom of expression. And while we have provisionally concluded that a definition of what is meant by a religious group is required, we have found it impossible to define "religion" or "religious" satisfactorily for this purpose. This is a matter upon which we welcome comment, particularly from those who believe they may be able to overcome these difficulties. But where arguments against provision of any offence are at least as substantial as those in its favour, we think that this further difficulty adds weight to the view that criminal sanctions should not be imposed.[422] Accordingly, and on the basis that we are proposing an offence penalising disturbances in places of religious worship,[423] we provisionally propose that the common law offences of blasphemy and blasphemous libel should be abolished and that there should be no statutory replacement. We recognise the arguments of substance which weigh against this conclusion, and invite comment upon and criticism of the range of arguments deployed in this Paper.

---

422 Compare Jones, "Blasphemy, Offensiveness and Law" (1980) B.J. Pol. S. 10, p. 148: "Imprecision is not at all unusual in law and often has to be accepted as inevitable if substantial harms are to be prevented. However, where the case for a law is finely balanced, the inability to state clearly what that law requires can be allowed to weigh against it".

423 See para. 12.16 et seq., below.

X POSSIBLE NON-CRIMINAL REMEDIES

10.1   If in accordance with our provisional proposals the present law of blasphemy were to be abolished and it was thought necessary to have some substitute for the common law, there remains the possibility of introducing or extending non-criminal remedies instead of providing a new criminal offence. In this connection it is relevant to recollect that the offence of incitement to racial hatred under section 5A of the Public Order Act 1936, introduced by section 70 of the Race Relations Act 1976, is only one element in the strategy of that Act designed to combat the problems of racial discrimination. It is noteworthy that by virtue of section 57 of that Act a person discriminated against in the fields of goods, services etc. has a claim in tort for damages or an injunction, and since blasphemy in its written form is a libel it is at any rate necessary to, raise the question whether such a remedy might usefully be made available.

10.2   For several reasons we doubt whether a civil remedy would be appropriate. The parallel with the position under the Race Relations Act 1976 is in our view no more valid in this respect than it is in the field of the criminal law: that Act, and the Sex Discrimination Act 1975, are designed to deal with special social problems which we consider have no parallel in the case of religious beliefs. Social and sexual discrimination may have tangible economic consequences, particularly in the spheres of employment and housing, which justify the civil remedies made available by those Acts; again, this consideration has no application in the sphere of attacks upon religious beliefs. Furthermore, quite apart from the inherent inappropriateness of the civil remedies of damages, or of the interlocutory injunction with its implications for freedom of expression, the nature of the conduct also appears to make civil remedies unsuitable. By contrast with the

position in racial or sexual discrimination, where the
civil remedies are designed to rectify individual cases
of discrimination, conduct is regarded as blasphemous
because it involves an attack on beliefs held in common
by a class of people. It is this distinction also which
makes it difficult to see how any remedy could be provided
analogous to that in defamatory libel. In English law no
action lies for defamation of a group: the matter
complained of must point personally to the individual
bringing the action.[424] That would not be so in the case
of matter intended to wound religious sensibilities in
general, and neither an individual nor a representative
action would appear to be appropriate. Further, what
would an action have to establish in any such case? In
defamation, it is injury to reputation, objectively
assessed. Words which merely injure feelings are not in
themselves considered sufficient to convey a defamatory
imputation;[425] but this would necessarily be of the
essence in any action for wounding of religious feelings.
It is difficult to see how this could be established
satisfactorily in practice.[426] Nevertheless, we welcome
comment upon the possibility of providing a civil remedy
if a suitable formulation can be produced.

---

424   Knupffer v. London Express Newspapers Limited [1944]
      A.C. 116; and see Orme v. Associated Newspapers Group
      Ltd., The Times, 4 February 1981.

425   Gatley on Libel and Slander (7th ed., 1974), para. 40.

426   The analogy with defamatory libel is even more
      difficult to sustain in the light of the
      recommendations of the Report of the Committee on
      Defamation (1975) Cmnd. 5909, under which defamation
      would be "publication to a third party of matter which
      in all the circumstances would be likely to affect a
      person adversely in the estimation of reasonable
      people generally", and for which a defence of "truth"
      would be substituted for the present defence of
      justification: see Report, pp. 172-173.

10.3   Finally we do not more than refer to the
possibility of greater use being made of the powers to
bind over individuals to keep the peace or be of good
behaviour; these powers are to be examined and reviewed
by us under a reference from the Lord Chancellor.[427] This
procedure would be available whether or not the criminal
law of blasphemy were to be abolished: it is not a
condition of its exercise that a criminal offence should
have been committed.[428] But while the power is still
widely used in situations concerned with breach of the
peace, it has been subject to severe criticism,[429] in
particular because it offends against the principle
nulla poena sine lege (none may be punished save for a
breach of the law). We make no proposals in relation to
it here, and suggest only that in situations where a
breach of the peace may reasonably be apprehended, and
where, therefore, an offence under section 5 of the Public
Order Act 1936 may be committed,[430] the binding over

---

427 The terms of reference are: "To examine the power to
     bind over to keep the peace and be of good behaviour
     under the Justices of the Peace Act 1361 and at
     common law together with related legislation, to
     consider whether such a power is needed and, if so,
     what its scope should be, and to recommend
     legislation accordingly, including such legislation
     upon procedural and any other matters as appear to be
     necessary in connection therewith".

428 See generally D.G.T. Williams, Keeping the Peace
     (1967), Ch. 4 and Stone's Justices' Manual (112th ed.,
     1980) pp. 568-572.

429 See Williams, op. cit.; Glanville Williams,
     "Preventive Justice and the Rule of Law" (1953)
     16 M.L.R. 417; (1969) 119 New L.J. p. 709. The
     Justices of the Peace Act 1361 (Amendment) Bill sought
     to limit the 1361 Act to cases brought before a court
     on a charge of an offence; the motion for leave to
     introduce it was negatived: Hansard (H.C.) 1978
     Vol. 951, cols. 45-52.

430 The situation in R. v. Gott (1922) 16 Cr. App. R. 87
     (see para. 2.14, above), where there was a public
     altercation, is an obvious example.

procedure offers an alternative means of dealing with the
dissemination of blasphemous matter.

10.4   This brief survey of non-criminal remedies
suggests that none of them would be satisfactory, or could
be made satisfactory, as a means of dealing with
blasphemous conduct, and we therefore do not propose the
use of such remedies in this context.

XI PROFANITY

A. The present law

11.1   We have mentioned already[431] that the City of
London Police Act 1839, the Metropolitan Police Act 1839
and, in similar but not identical terms, the Town Police
Clauses Act 1847, penalise anyone selling or exhibiting
to public view any "profane, indecent or obscene"
publication and anyone who "to the annoyance of the
inhabitants or passengers" sings any "profane, indecent
or obscene song or ballad" or uses any "profane, indecent
or obscene language". The first Act applies in the City
of London, the second in the Metropolitan Police
district,[432] the third elsewhere in England and Wales
where its provisions are specifically applied by other
Acts. There is little authority as to what is meant in
this context by "profane", except that it is not
synonymous with "indecent" or "obscene".[433] In every case
it must be established that there was actual annoyance,
even if only to one person.[434]

---

431 See para. 5.14, above; and see para. 5.6, n. 216.

432 See London Government Act 1963, s. 76.

433 Russon v. Dutton (No. 2) (1911) 104 L.T. 601, 602 per
     Hamilton J.: "I do not think that the word 'indecent'
     is to be taken eiusdem generis with 'profane' and
     'obscene'."

434 See Innes v. Newman [1894] 2 Q.B. 292 (local bye law
     penalising noise to the annoyance of inhabitants).

B. Provisional conclusion

11.2   We doubt if there is any need to retain the above-described provisions as to profane language or publication. So far as we are aware, prosecutions for public utterance of foul language are, whenever necessary, brought under section 5 of the Public Order Act 1936[435] or section 54(13) of the Metropolitan Police Act 1839, or local bye-laws. So far as publications are concerned, the legislation as to obscenity is the subject of the recent Report on Obscenity and Film Censorship.[436] Generally, we think that if, as we suggest, there is on balance no need for an offence dealing specifically with blasphemous conduct, this weakens the case for offences penalising language which falls short of blasphemy. Accordingly, we provisionally propose that the references to profanity in these offences should be repealed.

XII OFFENCES RELATING TO DISTURBANCES IN PLACES OF PUBLIC WORSHIP

A. Present Law

12.1   As in the case of blasphemy, there is a body of common law which relates to disturbance of public worship, but by contrast with blasphemy, statute law is now of far greater importance, even though some provisions relevant in this context have been repealed in recent years.[437] We deal in turn with the common law and with

---

435 See e.g. Simcock v. Rhodes (1977) 66 Cr. App. R. 192 and see para. 5.6, n. 216 as to other legislation in similar terms.

436 (1979) Cmnd. 7772; and see notes 242 and 246, above.

437 Toleration Act 1688, s. 15, repealed by the Statute Law (Repeals) Act 1969; Places of Religious Worship Act 1812, s. 12, repealed by the Courts Act 1971; and Religious Disabilities Act 1846, s. 4, repealed by the Statute Law (Repeals) Act 1977.

statutory provisions.

1. Common law

12.2   The precise breadth of the common law is
difficult to gauge. There are very broad statements in
Hawkins' Pleas of the Crown[438] to the effect that "all
irreverent behaviour" in churches and churchyards has
been regarded as criminal. More specifically there is
authority, by no means strong, for the propositions[439] that
it is an offence at common law -

> (a)   to disturb a priest of the established
>   Church in the performance of divine
>   worship,[440] and also, it seems, to
>   disturb Methodists and Dissenters when
>   engaged in their "decent and quiet
>   devotions";[441] and

> (b)   to strike any person in a church or
>   churchyard.[442]

12.3   The common law in this area has long ceased to
serve any useful purpose and, furthermore, is entirely
covered by the statutory provisions considered below. In

---

438   See 1 Hawk. c. 63, s. 23.

439   See Halsbury's Laws of England (4th ed., 1975) Vol. 14,
      para. 1050; Archbold (40th ed., 1979) para. 3411;
      Russell on Crime (12th ed., 1964) pp. 1525-7.

440   R. v. Parry (1686) Trem. P.C. 239; R. v. Wroughton
      (1765) 3 Burr. 1683, 97 E.R. 1045.

441   R. v. Wroughton, ibid., at p. 1684 per Lord Mansfield.

442   Wilson v. Greaves (1757) 1 Burr. 240, 243, 97 E.R. 293,
      295 per Lord Mansfield; and see Penhallo's Case
      (1590) Cro. Eliz. 231, 78 E.R. 487.

our view, it can be abolished.

2. Statute law

12.4   The offences relating to public worship in
churches, churchyards and burial grounds, are contained in
a number of statutes which we discuss in the following
paragraphs.

12.5   Section 59 of the Cemeteries Clauses Act 1847
imposes a maximum fine of £10[443] on anyone who -

    (a) plays any game or sport, or discharges
          firearms, save at a military funeral,
          in the cemetery; or

    (b) wilfully and unlawfully disturbs any
          persons assembled in the cemetery for the
          purpose of burying any body therein; or

    (c) commits any nuisance within the
          cemetery.[444]

---

443   Increased from £5 by the Criminal Justice Act 1967,
      Sch. 3.

444   By s. 1 the Act extends only to cemeteries authorised
      by subsequent Acts declaring it to be incorporated
      therewith. The Act was incorporated with many local
      Acts authorising the establishment of cemeteries and
      also temporarily with the Local Government Act 1972.
      The Act is, however, not now operative save in
      relation to a few cemetery companies. See Local
      Government Act 1972, s. 214 and Sch. 26, and the
      Local Authorities' Cemeteries Order 1977, S.I. 1977
      No. 204, referred to in para. 4.11, below.

12.6   Section 2 of the Ecclesiastical Courts
Jurisdiction Act 1860 penalises, in the first place, any
person guilty of "riotous, violent or indecent behaviour"
in any cathedral, church or chapel of the Church of England
or in any chapel of any religious denomination or in any
certified place of religious worship, "whether during the
celebration of divine service or at any other time", or in
any churchyard or burial ground; and secondly, any person
who shall "molest, let, disturb, vex, or trouble, or by
any other unlawful means disquiet or misuse" any preacher
duly authorised to preach therein or any clergyman in holy
orders ministering or celebrating any sacrament or any
divine service, rite or office. Offenders are liable on
summary conviction to a fine of £20 or imprisonment without
fine for two months[445] and an appeal lies to the Crown
Court.[446] Under section 3, the offender may, upon
commission of the offence, immediately and forthwith be
apprehended by any constable or churchwarden[447] of the
parish or place where the offence has been committed and
taken before a justice of the peace.

12.7   It will be noted that the offence under the
first part of section 2 of this Act ("the 1860 Act")
applies to conduct of the kind prohibited taking place in
Church of England buildings and in "any place of religious
worship duly certified under the provisions of the Places

---

445   Criminal Justice Act 1967 Sch. 3, Part I;
       Ecclesiastical Courts Jurisdiction Act 1860, s. 2.

446   Ecclesiastical Courts Jurisdiction Act 1860, s. 4;
       Courts Act 1971, ss. 8, 56(2), Sch. 1, Sch. 9,
       Part I.

447   As to the powers and duties of churchwardens in
       regard to disturbances of public worship, see
       Halsbury's Laws of England (4th ed., 1975) Vol. 14,
       para. 554 and Dale, The Law of the Parish Church
       (5th ed., 1975) pp. 92-94.

of Religious Worship Registration Act 1855".[448] Section 2
of the 1855 Act enables specified places of worship to be
certified in writing to the Registrar General of Births,
Marriages and Deaths through the superintendants of local
registries. The places of worship so specified include
those of "Protestant Dissenters or other Protestants",
"persons professing the Roman Catholic religion", "persons
professing the Jewish religion" and "every place of
meeting for religious worship of any other body or
denomination of persons". Section 10 of the 1855 Act
excludes Church of England places of worship; as we have
noted, specific provision is made for them by section 2
of the 1860 Act. Thus all certified places of worship, of
whatever religion, have the protection provided by the
offence under the 1860 Act. Certification will be effected
if the Registrar General is satisfied that the object of
the congregation is religious worship,[449] that the place
of meeting is used mainly for religious worship, and that
the congregation is an identifiable, settled body.[450]
"Worship" means having some at least of the characteristics
of "submission to the object worshipped, veneration of
that object, praise, thanksgiving, prayer or
intercession".[451]

---

448   The second part ("molesting" etc.) is limited to the
      Church of England.

449   See R. v. Registrar General. Ex. p. Segerdal (C.A.)
      [1970] 2 Q.B. 697, 706 per Lord Denning, M.R.

450   We are indebted to the General Register Office for
      information about the criteria applied.

451   Ibid., at p. 709 per Buckley L.J. A registered
      building is excepted from registration under the
      Charities Act 1960, is not liable to be rated, and
      may be registered for the solemnisation of marriages.
      Further, under s. 2 of the 1855 Act, the occupier of
      an unregistered building is liable to penalties if he
      permits worship in an unregistered building by more
      than 20 people unless (1) the meeting is in a private
      dwelling, or (2) the building is used only
      occasionally for this purpose; see Halsbury's Laws
      of England (4th ed., 1975) Vol. 14, para. 1411.

12.8   As we have noted, the offence in the 1860 Act
penalises any riotous, violent or "indecent"
behaviour in certified places of worship. "Indecent"
here has a specialised meaning to be ascertained from its
context in the statute. It is not referring to anything
in the nature of tending to corrupt or deprave, nor used
with any sexual connotation. It is used in the context
of "riotous, violent or indecent" behaviour, within
the genus of creating a disturbance in a sacred place.
Thus there was held to be indecent behaviour when there
were interruptions (shouts of "Oh, you hypocrites; how
can you use the word of God to justify your policies?")
during a church service attended by members of the
Government, their theme being a protest against Government
members' participation in the service against a background
of alleged support for United States' policies in
Vietnam.[452] Charges under section 5 of the Public Order
Act 1936 were presumably thought inappropriate because
in the circumstances of a religious service no breach of
the peace was likely to be occasioned. Whether or not
behaviour is indecent is a question of fact for the
court.[453]

12.9   Section 36 of the Offences against the Person
Act 1861 imposes a maximum penalty of two years'
imprisonment on anyone who –

> (a) by threats or force, obstructs or
>   prevents or endeavours to obstruct

---

452   Abrahams v. Cavey [1968] 1 Q.B. 479.

453   R. v. Farrant [1973] Crim. L.R. 240 (Middlesex Crown
      Court, on appeal from justices): held an offence
      under the Act where persons were using "magic"
      symbols and incantations to try to raise the dead in
      an Anglican churchyard at midnight.

or prevent, any clergyman or other
minister in or from (i) celebrating
divine service or otherwise officiating
in any church, chapel, meeting house
or other place of divine worship, or
(ii) performing his duty in the lawful
burial of the dead in any churchyard
or other burial place;   or

(b)   strikes or offers any violence to or,
on any civil process, under pretence
of executing such process, arrests
any clergyman or other minister
engaged in, or to the offender's
knowledge about to engage in, any of
the rites or duties referred to in (a),
above, or who to the offender's
knowledge is going to or returning
from the performance thereof.[454]

There is no authority as to whether a "place of divine
worship" under this section is to be construed more
narrowly than a "place of worship" in the Places of
Religious Worship Registration Act 1855, but it is in any
event clear that the offence under section 2 of the
Ecclesiastical Courts Jurisdiction Act 1860, in covering
"riotous" etc. behaviour at any time, is of wider
application than this offence. Section 36 has been
recommended for repeal without replacement by the Criminal
Law Revision Committee.[455]

---

454   The draft Criminal Code of 1879, s. 142 is based on
      this section and similar provisions are to be found
      in some Commonwealth codes based on the 1879 draft;
      see e.g. Canadian Criminal Code, s. 172.

455   14th Report, Offences against the Person (1980)
      Cmnd. 7844, paras. 179-180.

12.10 Section 7 of the Burial Laws Amendment Act 1880 penalises any person[456] -

   (a)   guilty of any riotous, violent or indecent behaviour at any burial under the Act, or wilfully obstructing such burial or any burial service; and

   (b)   in any churchyard or graveyard in which parishioners have a right of burial (section 1), who delivers any address, not being part of or incidental to a religious service and not otherwise permitted by any lawful authority, or who wilfully endeavours to bring into contempt or obloquy the Christian religion, or the belief or worship of any church or denomination of Christians, or its members or minister, or any other person.

12.11 Section 214 of the Local Government Act 1972 specifies the burial authorities who may provide and maintain cemeteries. "Cemetery" here includes a burial ground or any other place set aside for the interment of the dead, including any part of such a place set aside for the interment of ashes.[457] The Secretary of State may

---

456 By virtue of the Powers of Criminal Courts Act 1973 s. 18(1), he is punishable with a maximum of two years' imprisonment.

457 Sect. 214(8). The burial authorities are the councils of districts, London boroughs, parishes and communities, the Common Council of the City of London, the parish meetings of parishes having no parish council, and also joint boards established under the Public Health Act 1936, s. 6 or by or under local Acts for the provision and maintenance of cemeteries.

by order provide for their management, regulation and control, and impose a fine for contravening an order.[458] The current order[459] prohibits nuisances or wilful disturbances in a cemetery; wilful interference with any burials taking place in a cemetery, or with any grave, vault, tombstone or other memorial and flowers thereon; and games and sports in a cemetery. "Burial" here includes the chapels provided on any part of them.[460] Persons contravening the order are liable on summary conviction to a £100 fine and, in the case of a continuing offence, to £10 for each day during which the offence continues after conviction.

12.12   It should also be noted that charges under section 1 of the Criminal Damage Act 1971, penalising criminal damage with maximum penalty of ten years' imprisonment and a fine, may also be brought in appropriate circumstances where there is more serious damage to churches, chapels or other places of worship, or cemeteries and the memorials etc. which they contain.[461]

B. Proposals for reform

1. Disturbances in places of worship

(a) General considerations

12.13   We have already proposed that the common law in this area be abolished, as it long ago fell into total

---

458   Sect. 214(3).

459   The Local Authorities' Cemeteries Order 1977, S.I. 1977 No. 204; see Articles 18-19.

460   See Articles 2(2) and 6.

461   If the total value of the property destroyed is below £200, the defendant is to be tried summarily: Criminal Law Act 1977, s. 23 and Sch. 4 (Magistrates' Courts Act 1980, s. 22 and Sch. 2).

desuetude. So far as the statutory offences are concerned,
it is plain that, in addition to the somewhat outmoded
language in which those described in paragraphs 12.5-12.10
are cast, there is a considerable overlap between them. The
overlapping of section 36 of the Offences against the
Person Act 1861 and section 2 of the Ecclesiastical Courts
Jurisdiction Act 1860 has been noted.[462] In addition,
since the latter covers "riotous, violent or indecent
behaviour" in any burial ground (not in terms restricted
in any way), there seems to be a considerable overlap with
the two offences in the Cemeteries Clauses Act 1847 and the
Burial Laws Amendment Act 1880.

12.14   The Criminal Law Revision Committee has
recommended that section 36 of the Offences against the
Person Act 1861 be repealed without any specially tailored
offence to take its place. We agree with the Committee,
and we also agree with them that a general offence of common
assault is all that is needed in this context.[463] The
questions which we have to consider are whether the offences
other than those contained in recent legislation outlined
in paragraphs 12.11-12.12 may be dispensed with similarly,
and if so whether it is appropriate to propose their
repeal in the present context.

12.15   The second part of the offence under section 2
of the Ecclesiastical Courts Jurisdiction Act 1860, dealing
with the "molesting" etc. of clergymen, is, like section 36
of the Offences against the Person Act 1861, a special form
of assault or threatened assault. To this extent, the
offence seems unnecessary in modern conditions, and
provisionally we propose that it be repealed without

---

462 See para. 12.9, above.

463 The C.L.R.C. recommend that an offence of assault
     be retained with summary trial: 14th Report,
     Offences against the Person (1980) Cmnd. 7844,
     paras. 158-165.

replacement. The first part of this offence,[464] however, penalising "riotous, violent or indecent behaviour", is far wider and, although persons indulging in such behaviour could no doubt be bound over to keep the peace as an alternative to prosecution, there seems to be no other offence which is tailored to meet the conduct with which it deals.[465] As we have noted,[466] that conduct extends to any behaviour which is "indecent", in the sense of being improper in the particular place in which it occurs. We do not think that reliance can be placed purely on the binding over procedure.[467] Repeal of this part of the section would therefore necessitate its replacement, at least in part. We have considered whether it is appropriate to propose this here. The difficulty lies in the present interconnection between section 2 of the 1860 Act and Canon Law. We have noted[468] the powers of churchwardens in regard to offences under section 2. The correlative duties of churchwardens include the maintenance of order and decorum; and those duties, in the event of disturbance, are under Canon Law[469] defined

---

464 See para. 12.6, above.

465 Sect. 5 of the Public Order Act 1936 may be inapplicable for the reason given in para. 12.8, above, and also if the particular place of worship is not one to which the general public "have or are permitted to have access": see definition of "public place" in s. 9(1), as substituted by the Criminal Justice Act 1972, s. 33, para. 5.7, n. 219, above. Furthermore, it is not a condition of certification under the Places of Religious Worship Registration Act 1855 that the place of meeting is used for public religious worship; only if registration is required of a building for solemnisation of marriage under the Marriage Acts 1949-1970 must the worship be public.

466 See para. 12.8, above.

467 See para. 10.3, above; see also Robilliard, "Religious Freedom as Part of a Bill of Rights" (1979) Law & Justice No. 60-61, p. 8 at pp. 12-13.

468 See para. 12.6 and n. 447, above.

469 See the authorities quoted in n. 447, above.

in terms modelled precisely on the language of section 2
of the 1860 Act. Thus replacement of section 2 may
necessitate changes in Canon Law, which is outside our
terms of reference. Nevertheless, on balance we believe
it to be preferable to take this opportunity to modernise
this criminal offence, particularly since the authorities
indicate that its interpretation is not free from
difficulty.

(b) A new offence

12.16   We turn now to the requirements of a new
offence. Those requirements cannot be formulated without
first stating the needs which the offence would answer.
We have already noted that the legislation relating to
public order may be inappropriate to deal with disturbances
in places of worship, and the provision of a specific
offence covering such conduct may avoid the distortion in
the interpretation of that legislation (in particular,
section 5 of the Public Order Act 1936)[470] which might
otherwise ensue were it to be invoked in situations which
on their facts might not give rise to any likelihood of a
disturbance of the public peace. In addition, while we
find serious difficulties in justifying an offence in this
sphere applying to activities in public places in general
which goes beyond the bounds of the present law relating
to public order, it is easier to justify a more restricted
offence which would apply solely in places of worship
where people go for meditation and prayer as well as
communal worship.[471] Furthermore, there is some evidence
that such an offence is needed. We have been referred to

---

470 See para. 5.6, above.
471 See paras. 7.18 and 7.22-7.23, above.

a recent instance[472] in which two people were fined after
depositing the head of a pig in a mosque while a group
of Muslims were present. This caused immediate anger
amongst the local Muslim community, and proceedings were
accordingly taken under section 5 of the Public Order Act
1936. But it is not difficult to postulate such conduct,
or equivalent conduct, occurring in premises belonging to
any faith, which are empty at the time, so that no breach
of the peace may occur, and where no damage is done to
the building or to its contents but where the users of
the building would feel that a deliberate act of
desecration had taken place. In such circumstances a
specially designed offence seems desirable.

12.17   The principal elements of the offence may in our
view best be expressed simply as the use of threatening,
abusive or insulting words or behaviour at any time in a
certified place of worship. We are aware that the terms
"threatening, abusive or insulting" have an ancestry at
least as venerable as the terms at present used in the
offence under section 2 of the 1860 Act,[473] and we have
therefore considered whether some alternative, such as
"violent or offensive", might be more appropriate today.
Provisionally, however, we think the former to be
preferable. The terms were only recently adopted once more
in the offence of incitement to racial hatred introduced
in 1976, which forms section 5A of the Public Order Act
1936,[474] where to this extent they form a parallel to
section 5 of that Act. Furthermore, while it is difficult
to postulate forms of "violent" behaviour which would not

---

472   This occurred in a mosque at Batley Carr in 1980;
      the case is reported in the Dewsbury Reporter, 12
      September 1980. See also Law Society's Gazette,
      21 January 1981, p. 60 for an account of reported
      disruptions by hooligans of traditional Christmas
      midnight church services.

473   See n. 216, above.

474   See para. 5.9, above.

in any event constitute an offence against person or
property, "threatening, abusive or insulting" words or
behaviour seem to us wide enough to cover the full range
of non-violent conduct which the offence should be
designed to include, such as offensive interruptions to
services, as in Abrahams v. Cavey,[475] distribution or
affixing of objectionable written material, or conduct
such as occurred in the incident in a mosque described in
the preceding paragraph, whether or not others are present
at the time.

12.18   Provisionally we propose that the new offence
should apply in the premises and places specified in
section 2 of the Ecclesiastical Courts Jurisdiction Act
1860,[476] that is, in any cathedral, church or chapel of
the Church of England or in any certified place of
religious worship, or in any churchyard or burial ground.
It would therefore cover synagogues, mosques, Hindu temples
and all other certified places of worship of whatever
religion. Ideally, it might be preferable to extend the
application to any place of religious worship, but this
would pose difficulties. Some places of worship are not
certified and are simply rooms set aside for that purpose
within private houses,[477] and it seems to us inappropriate
that the offence which we propose should extend to private
houses. Secondly, without the criterion of certification
the difficulties of defining what is meant by "religion"
or "religious" which we have examined at length earlier
in this Paper[478] would again present themselves. The
criterion of certification, if not ideal, is at any rate
well settled and readily ascertainable in any given case.

---

475 [1968] 1 Q.B. 479; see para. 12.8, above.
476 See para. 12.6, above.
477 See n. 451, above.
478 See paras. 8.15-8.22, above.

12.19   Two elements of the proposed offence remain for
consideration: whether it should have some kind of mental
element or specific defences, and the mode of trial and
penalties. To some extent the answer to the first issue
depends on the mode of trial and maximum penalty, since
were the offence to be triable only summarily, with the
maximum sentence which can be imposed by a magistrates'
court,[479] we would be less inclined to favour the addition
of a mental element. In our provisional view, however,
the offence should be capable of being tried on indictment,
having regard to the serious consequences for the community
produced by the worst examples of the kinds of incidents
with which the offence is intended to deal. The most
closely comparable offence might be thought to be that
under section 5A of the Public Order Act 1936 (incitement
to racial hatred),[480] which when tried on indictment has
a maximum penalty of two years' imprisonment and a fine.
We bear in mind, however, that in the short period when
the offence under section 5 of the Public Order Act
(insulting behaviour likely to lead to a breach of the
peace) was triable on indictment,[481] the maximum term of
imprisonment was 12 months, a period which we also suggest
in this Paper for a possible offence to penalise the
wounding or outraging of religious feelings.[482] Bearing
in mind also that the offence under consideration is not
intended to deal with actual violence to the person or
damage to property, we provisionally propose that the
offence should be triable either way, that is, either
summarily or on indictment, and that the maximum penalty on

---

479   Six months' imprisonment and a fine of £1000: see
      Criminal Law Act 1977, ss. 27 et seq. (Magistrates'
      Courts Act 1980, ss. 31 et seq.).

480   See para. 5.9, above.

481   I.e. between 1963-1977; see para. 5.6, above.

482   See para. 8.24, above.

indictment should be 12 months' imprisonment and a fine.

12.20   If, as we propose, the offence is to be triable
on indictment with penalties more severe than those
available in magistrates' courts, we think that it would
be desirable to provide at the very least certain defences,
or alternatively a mental element. The defences would,
we suggest, provide that the defendant should not be guilty
if he were to show that he did not know that the place
concerned was a place of worship etc., and/or secondly,
that he did not know or could not reasonably have been
expected to know that what he did was likely to wound or
outrage the feelings of those using the place of worship.
This would be a less stringent requirement for the
prosecution to overcome than a full mental element.
However, if as we suggest the offence is to be triable on
indictment, we incline to the view that such an element
is desirable; we think that the appropriate mental
element would be an intent to wound or outrage the feelings
of those using the place of worship in question. We
invite views on whether an extra element in the shape
either of defences or a mental element should be included
in the proposed offence, and what form that element should
take.

2.   Disturbances in burial grounds

12.21   The old statutory offences relating specifically
to disturbances in cemeteries are of limited utility.
Apparently the Cemeteries Clauses Act 1847 now applies only
to a very few companies authorised by other legislation
to construct a cemetery. As for cemeteries and crematoria
managed by local authorities, the provisions outlined in
paragraph 12.11, above effectively supersede those of the
Burial Laws Amendment Act 1880. This Act does, however,
apply also to Church of England churchyards, and to that

extent the offence in section 7[483] is still relevant.
But we have noted above that the offence in the first
part of section 2 of the Ecclesiastical Courts
Jurisdiction Act 1860 applies in "any churchyard or burial
ground", which presumably includes not only Church of
England churchyards, but those belonging to Methodists
and any other non-Church of England churches, as well as
private burial grounds and burial grounds managed by
companies under the 1847 Act. We have proposed the
replacement of this part of section 2 of the 1860 Act with
an offence having the same broad application. We think
that this offence would be sufficiently wide to make
unnecessary the offence in section 7 of the Burial Laws
Amendment Act 1880. Accordingly, we provisionally propose
the repeal of this section and of section 59 of the
Cemeteries Clauses Act 1847.

C. Summary of provisional proposals

12.22   Of the old offences relating to disturbances of
public worship, we consider that only the first part of
section 2 of the Ecclesiastical Courts Jurisdiction Act
1860 still retains a useful function, although it is
archaic in its language. We provisionally propose that
it should be replaced by an offence similar in scope but
in modernised language. This would be an indictable
offence triable either way, with a maximum sentence of
12 months' imprisonment and a fine. It would penalise
anyone who, with intent to wound and outrage the feelings
of those using the premises concerned, uses threatening,
abusive or insulting words or behaviour at any time in
any place of worship of the Church of England, in any

---

483 See para. 12.10, above.

other certified place of religious worship[484] or in any churchyard or burial ground (paragraphs 12.17-12.20).

12.23   The other old offences, both statutory and common law, seem to us no longer to serve any useful purpose, and we provisionally propose their abolition or repeal. These are -

   1.   the common law offences of disturbing a priest at divine worship and striking anyone in a church or churchyard (paragraphs 12.2-12.3);

   2.   the Cemeteries Clauses Act 1847, section 59 (paragraphs 12.5 and 12.20);

   3.   the second part of section 2 of the Ecclesiastical Courts Jurisdiction Act 1860, dealing with assaults and threatened assaults on the clergy (paragraphs 12.6 and 12.15);

   4.   section 36 of the Offences against the Person Act 1861 (which has already been recommended for repeal by the Criminal Law Revision Committee)[485] (paragraphs 12.9 and 12.14);   and

   5.   the Burial Laws Amendment Act 1880, section 7 (paragraphs 12.10 and 12.21).

---

484   I.e. certified under the Places of Religious Worship Registration Act 1855: see para. 12.7, above. Thus, provided that they are certified, the offence would cover synagogues, mosques, Hindu temples and places of worship belonging to any other religion.

485   14th Report, Offences against the Person (1980) Cmnd. 7844, paras. 179-180.

13.1   In relation to blasphemy, we provisionally
propose the abolition without replacement of the common
law offences of blasphemy and blasphemous libel. The
principal reasons which have led us to this conclusion may
be summarised as follows -

      A.   The common law offences of blasphemy and
            blasphemous libel possess serious defects
            and it is in any event necessary to
            abolish them as part of the process of
            codifying the criminal law (paragraphs
            1.2 and 6.1-6.11).

      B.   In so far as blasphemous conduct is
            concerned with public order, existing
            legislation, including in particular
            section 5 of the Public Order Act
            1936,[486] is capable of dealing with
            many situations which are likely to arise,
            and the requirements of public order are
            not a sufficiently strong ground for
            retaining criminal offences to deal
            solely with blasphemous conduct. There
            is in addition a wide range of other
            offences capable of dealing with some
            forms of blasphemous conduct (paragraphs
            5.3, 5.6, 5.14-5.15 and 7.22-7.23).

      C.   Criminal sanctions upon blasphemous
            conduct are otherwise best justified upon
            the basis that such conduct involves

---

486   This penalises threatening, abusive and insulting
      behaviour in public places; see further para. 5.6,
      above.

public insults which wound or outrage
the feelings of religious believers;
such feelings are arguably unique in
character and thus deserve protection
(paragraphs 7.12-7.21).

D.   But at least equal weight must be given
to countervailing considerations, such
as the possibility that criminal sanctions
might involve unacceptable limitations
upon freedom of expression, the fact that
there seem to be few public expressions
of hostility to religious beliefs and
that consequently there are no social
tensions corresponding to those which gave
rise to the need for the race relations
legislation (paragraphs 7.5-7.21).

E.   In addition to the considerations referred
to in (D), there seem to be severe
obstacles to the satisfactory formulation
of an offence to penalise the wounding
and outraging of feelings of the adherents
of any religious group. In particular,
while it is necessary to define what is
meant by "religious" or "religion" in
this context, there seem to be
insurmountable difficulties in devising
a satisfactory definition of these terms.
This difficulty must be allowed to weigh
against the need for criminal sanctions,
and, bearing in mind also the
considerations in (D) above, we
provisionally conclude that we should
propose no new offence to deal with
blasphemous conduct (paragraphs 7.24-7.26,
8.1-8.25 and 9.1-9.2).

F.   The provision of new non-criminal
      remedies would be inappropriate
      (paragraphs 10.1-10.4).

13.2   In relation to profanity, we provisionally
conclude that references to profanity in old legislation
should be repealed, principally because prosecutions for
the public utterance of objectionable language are,
whenever required, brought under more recent legislation
such as section 5 of the Public Order Act 1936.   These
references appear in section 35(12) of the City of London
Police Act 1839, section 54(12) of the Metropolitan Police
Act 1839, and section 28 of the Town Police Clauses Act
1847[487] (paragraph 11.2).

13.3   In relation to disturbances in places of public
worship we provisionally propose that, in place of the
offence at present contained in the first part of section 2
of the Ecclesiastical Courts Jurisdiction Act 1860,[488]
there should be a new offence penalising anyone who, with
intent to wound or outrage the feelings of those using the
premises concerned, uses threatening, abusive or insulting
words or behaviour at any time in any place of worship
of the Church of England, in any other certified place of

---

487 These offences penalise with low maximum fines
     "profane, indecent or obscene" publications,
     language and songs etc; see further paras. 5.14 and
     11.11, above.

488 This penalises with a maximum sentence of two months'
     imprisonment or a fine of £20 "riotous, violent or
     indecent behaviour" in any Church of England place of
     worship, in any other certified place of worship
     (see n. 489, below) or in any churchyard or burial
     ground; see further, para. 12.6, above.

religious worship,[489] in any churchyard or burial ground.
The offence should be triable either summarily or on
indictment with a maximum sentence on indictment of 12
months' imprisonment and a fine (paragraphs 12.17-12.20).
Other old offences in this area now serve no useful purpose
and we provisionally propose their abolition or repeal
(paragraphs 12.13-12.15 and 12.21).

13.4   The proposals in this Working Paper are
provisional in character, and we welcome comment upon and
criticism both of these proposals and of the arguments
considered and the provisional conclusions reached in all
parts of the Paper.

---

489 I.e. certified under section 2 of the Places of
     Religious Worship Registration Act 1855. Under this
     section places of worship of all religions may be
     certified as such if the Registrar General of Births,
     Marriages and Deaths is satisfied as to certain
     conditions. Thus, provided that they are certified,
     this offence would protect synagogues, mosques, Hindu
     temples and places of worship belonging to any other
     religion.

Printed in England for Her Majesty's Stationery Office
by Robendene Ltd, Amersham
Dd 718931 C18 3/81